W9-AEI-985

THE VOCATION OF LADY CHRISTINE

THE VOCATION OF *Lady Christine*

SISTER EBLANA, O.D.C.

"Sanctity is an adventure."
— Bernanos

THE BRUCE PUBLISHING COMPANY • MILWAUKEE

NIHIL OBSTAT:

JOHN F. MURPHY, S.T.D.
Censor librorum

IMPRIMATUR:

✠ WILLIAM E. COUSINS
Archbishop of Milwaukee

January 13, 1964

Library of Congress Catalog Card Number: 64–17408

To the memory of
MOTHER THERESE O'BRIEN, O.D.C.,
fervent admirer of
the French Carmel

THE VOCATION OF LADY CHRISTINE

Chapter 1

No one acquainted with the life and reign of King Henry the Fourth of France would expect to find a granddaughter of his in a Carmelite convent; mysticism is not usually associated with the House of Bourbon. More, the spiritual legacy left by a man who changed his religion three times from ambitious motives ought in the nature of things to have produced little better than religious indifference. However, in religious history it is often the unexpected that happens. The daughter he had by La Belle d'Estrées and legitimatized with the name Gabrielle de France and the title Duchess de la Valette inherited none of the weaknesses of either of her parents. On the contrary, even as a young girl she shunned the company of pleasure-seekers and gravitated as it were, instinctively to the elite of the Court, those ladies who, sincerely religious, understood their obligations to both God and neighbor.

In the first decades of the seventeenth century, the poor in Paris were as numerous and as neglected as at any other period, and there were no Sisters of Charity or food centers to supply their needs. This great want was met by a group of women, many of them of noble rank, who gave their services and their wealth without stint. Being of royal birth,

Duchess Gabrielle could not take part personally in this good work but she made up by bountiful almsgiving and by unflagging interest in every project undertaken by them.

In 1622 Gabrielle married a young aristocrat, Bernard, son and heir of Henry de Nogaret, Duke of Epernon. Husband and wife had little in common. Whereas Gabrielle took a serious view of her duties as a Christian to others, Bernard concentrated all his attention on himself. With singleness of purpose worthy of a higher end he devoted all his talents, wealth, and influence to the pursuit of his own advancement in life. His vast estates and vaster ambitions occupied his mind to the exclusion of all else; yet when adversity struck he took it like a man and won the respect of his enemies by his refusal to have any truck with intriguers.

They were married two years when Gabrielle gave birth to her first baby, a girl. How pleased would the mother have been, how proud the father, could they have foreknown that this child was destined to become so distinguished a member of the Carmelite Order that a full-length biography of her would appear in each of the three centuries after her death.

The public baptism of the infant brought together an illustrious gathering, the sponsors being King Louis the Thirteenth, his Queen, Anne of Austria, and his sister Christine, Duchess of Savoy. In their honor she was christened Anne-Louise-Christine, and her surnames on the register read: de Foix de la Valette d'Epernon.

Following the example of her intimate friends, Queen Marie de Medici and Queen Anne of Austria, Duchess Gabrielle had been accustomed to pay visits at regular intervals to the community in the Monastery of the Incarnation in the district of St. Jacques, the first Carmel founded in France; so when her baby was six weeks old she had it taken there to be prayed over by the famous Prioress, the Venerable Magdalen of St. Joseph. This great nun, known in her day as the St. Teresa of France, carried the infant to the choir and, holding it in her arms, knelt for quite a long time, doubtless entreating – and obtaining – from God the almost miraculous graces that in years to come would bring Christine the spiritual strength to prefer the title Sister Anne-Marie to that of Queen of Poland.

Within a year the child fell sick and came near dying. The mother, distraught at the thought of losing her child, invoked the aid of St. Francis of Paula and promised that if the baby was restored to health she would dedicate it to God. Her petition was granted. The grown woman Christine, when recalling this answer to prayer, used to say with a wry smile that although duly grateful for St. Francis' interest in her welfare she would have been doubly thankful to him had he let her fly away to heaven, a holy innocent twelve months old.

She was still but a small child when her mother died, shortly after the birth of a son. As her end drew near the holy Duchess sent for Christine to bid her a last farewell. At the sight of the little tear-stained face the mother felt her courage falter before the terrible sacrifice demanded of her by the will of God and asked to have her taken away.

Scarcely three years old, Christine was too young to realize the depth of her loss, but as the months succeeded one another her loving heart found some consolation in gazing at the baby brother, who was fast attaining a marked resemblance to his mother.

Though she missed her mother she was not at all given to sadness; in fact she was blessed with good spirits, and her happy temperament endeared her to all who had charge of her.

Graceful as a fairy, dark-haired and dark-eyed, she had not, however, inherited her mother's beauty; but her dainty appearance, her agreeable disposition, and her readiness to enter into conversation with her elders made her an attractive little companion, pleasant both to look at and to listen to.

Seldom are a brother and sister more attached to each other than were Christine and Jean. Throughout their childhood they were inseparable; even when playing happily with other children they liked to be near each other.

Queen Anne, who had always numbered the Duchess Gabrielle among her dearest friends, now loved her in her children. She took an almost maternal interest in both of them, showed genuine concern for their well-being and often had Christine accompany her on her visits to the Carmelites. On these occasions the Venerable Magdalen never failed to take the child aside to give her little talks on the love of God and little lessons in the art of pleasing Him. This instruction continued for years and did not go unheeded. One morning when returning with the Queen from Mass Christine was invited by her to get into her carriage. As she was eagerly hoisting herself up the steep step she got a violent push from one of the young maids of honor consumed with jealousy on account of the royal favor shown her and would have fallen backward onto the street had not the officer in attendance happened to be standing directly behind her and caught her in his arms. The Queen, not having seen the rough thrust given by the jealous girl, cried out in alarm and said in a tone of vexation: "Christine, what an awkward child you are!" Christine blushed at the rebuke but, choking back the excuse that sprang to her lips, replied: "Yes, your Majesty, I will be more careful next time."

Another incident throws more light on her character. Once when on her way to the Queen's apartments she was stopped by a group of men standing together in one of the long galleries. The oldest of them bowed respectfully to her and, saying that his friends had a favor to ask of her, pressed a large sum of money into her hand. "We know that her Majesty can refuse you nothing," he said. "Will you then be so good as to ask her to grant us the privilege of putting an impost on wine?" To be treated as an influential personage by elderly businessmen was a highly flattering experience for thirteen-year-old Christine. Without a moment's hesitation she pocketed the gold coins and went straight to the Queen with the request, which was readily granted. That evening, delighted to have such an interesting experience to her credit, she entertained her brother and his tutor with a full account of this, her first financial transaction. The priest listened to her with an air of deep dissatisfaction and then said: "You don't understand what you have done. Not only have you accepted a bribe, but by procuring that privilege you will have taken away the livelihood of countless small shopkeepers. That money you were given is the blood of the poor." Christine, dumbfounded at this revelation of the harm she had done so unwittingly resolved to undo it without delay. She lost no time in obtaining an audience with the Queen who, on hearing Christine's report of the tutor's denunciation, was, like her, filled with remorse and promised to have the permission canceled that very day.

Her life followed the routine of the aristocratic young girl of the period. She was under the authority of two governesses, both of them noblewomen; and with her equable, docile character she got on well with them. Her contact with royalty was confined to accompanying them on what might be called religious outings; attendance at Mass on the chief festivals, visits to two or three convents of Carmelites and of Visitandines, and pilgrimages to shrines within easy reach of Paris.

These few items apart, very little is recorded of her childhood. She kept up her visits to the Carmel even after the death of the Venerable Magdalen and, for a motherless girl, was exceptionally devout and well instructed in her religion. These visits, however, far from inspiring her with the desire to spend her life in the cloister, had the opposite effect. At the end of twenty minutes she was glad to take leave of the nuns and get away from the thought of them and their double grilles and locked doors.

She was little more than a child when her father's preoccupied air and his long absences from Paris prepared her for the news that things were not going well with him. Each day he became more and more painfully aware of the precariousness of his position at Court. Watching with sinking heart the rise to supreme power of Cardinal Richelieu, he gave little thought to the welfare of his children. His forebodings of disaster were only too well founded. Being a man of considerable influence he got in Richelieu's way, with the result that the Cardinal Minister contrived his downfall on a trumped-up charge of culpable negligence in his military duties at the siege of Fontarabie. Sentenced to banishment for life, deprived of his title, and stripped of his possessions, Duke Bernard took refuge, like most of his companions in misfortune, at the English Court where they were sure of a welcome from the consort of Charles the First, Queen Henrietta (who was a daughter of Henry the Fourth of France). Many months earlier, apprised of Richelieu's machinations, he had anticipated the Cardinal's move by having the greater part of his immense fortune conveyed in secret to London. This explains how, when there, he was able to lend the impoverished King of England the large sum of six hundred thousand livres.

Shortly after their father's banishment Christine and her brother were sent for by their grandfather to come and live with him. He, too, had suffered at the hands of Richelieu.

Convinced that the old Duke was hostile to him, the all-powerful Minister had had him banished from Court with orders not to leave his ancestral estates in Guyenne. The presence of the children, both of them well behaved and affectionate, must have relieved the intolerable tedium of his long, lonely days when, oppressed by solitude and in failing health, he had ample grounds for meditating on the fickleness of fortune. The tragedy of his later years was all the more poignant in contrast to the brilliant promise of his early manhood when he had been the friend and favorite of King Henry the Third. But Richelieu's assumption of absolute power had put an end to his hopes and ambitions and at less than sixty years of age, the Duke had been forced to retire for good to his estates in the south, far from the great capital where his heart lay.

The serious conversation of the old man had its effect on the young girl. Sympathetic by nature she entered into his feelings as he relived in anecdote the triumphs of his youth, abruptly succeeded by the catastrophes of his mature years. With so attentive a listener at his side, the old Duke never tired of descanting upon the vicissitudes of a courtier's life and always concluded with the recital of his wrongs and grievances so that at times his melancholy proved infectious and descended like a cloud upon Christine's sensitive heart.

She was his last human consolation. Before a year had passed even Christine's inexperienced eyes could see he was fast approaching the grave. To the last day of his life he could think and speak of nothing but his personal woes, the galling humiliations he had suffered under Richelieu and the crushing sense of failure that had broken his spirit and robbed him of the courage to live.

Duke Bernard, on hearing of his father's death, ordered Christine to join him in London. The prospect of such a journey at such a time would have daunted the stoutest heart. Half submissive, half reluctant, Christine set out and with every mile of the road felt a growing sense of depression at the thought of living in a country still enduring the bitterness of religious persecution. It was the year 1640. Charles the First was on the throne. Queen Henrietta and her immediate circle enjoyed the gracious permission of the English government to practice their religion, but only in private.

Christine's two years in London brought her a new and priceless experience: a closeup view of Catholics under persecution. Controversy was in the air. At the religious disputations held in the open places of the city one Church was always under attack, the Old Church. Christine, though her contacts were necessarily confined to a small group, could see that this polemical warfare, far from undermining the faith of sincere Catholics, only strengthened their attachment to the Pope and to all he stood for. Her own love of her Church drew new life and warmth from contact with Catholics who, valiant confessors of the Old Religion, deemed it a privilege to suffer for their beliefs.

A not uncommon spectacle in the London of that time which she watched with wide-eyed fascination from the safe vantage point of her window made a lasting impression on her. It was an anti-Catholic demonstration. Shouting at the top of their voices: "To the gallows with the Papists!" a frenzied mob went running through the street, their wild and menacing looks betokening the pitiless zeal with which they would make good their threat, given the chance. Terrified and yet thrilled at this sight Christine flung herself prostrate on the floor and offered her life to Jesus Christ, protesting she would be only too glad to suffer torture and death for His sake. This was the incident that gave birth to her devotion to the virgin-martyrs, and throughout her stay in England hardly a day passed without her petitioning these saints to obtain for her the grace of winning some day a crown like theirs.

In 1642 the announcement of Richelieu's death came to Duke Bernard. With grim satisfaction he wound up his affairs in England and hurried back to France. On reaching Paris he immediately embarked on the undertaking of the first importance to him, the procurement of full rehabilitation. In order to vindicate his honor he, the Duke of Epernon, made himself a voluntary prisoner in the Conciergerie Jail, convinced that this was the only way of getting a just hearing of his case and of having his name forever cleared. Without undue delay the Parliament made a thorough investigation of his affair, with the happiest results. His good name was recovered, his title and estates restored, and, as for Christine, she was readmitted to the good graces of the Queen and could look forward to taking her rightful place in society.

Chapter 2

Duke Bernard celebrated his restoration to fortune by entering upon a second marriage, his bride being none other than Marie de Chambout, niece of his old adversary, Cardinal Richelieu. Happily for all concerned she bore no resemblance to her uncle. On the contrary, like his other niece, the saintly Duchess d'Aiguillon, she was a lovable woman and, on taking her place at her husband's side, she showed herself a true mother to her stepchildren.

A new life opened for Christine, now eighteen years old. As granddaughter of Henry the Fourth she was welcome everywhere, in even the most exclusive circles. In no time she found herself accepted as an equal, and in fact, as a cherished friend by young women, bearers of glittering names such as de Montpensier, de Guise, de Montmorency, de Rohan, etc. The swift transition from obscurity to recognition on this scale proved too much for her. Dazzled by the elegance and charm of these ladies, she thought of them from morning till night. In her young eyes they were goddesses, models to be copied in every way and at all costs. Before many months had passed they occupied the place in her heart once held by the virgin-martyrs.

The glamor of Court life held her spellbound. The almost sacred awe surrounding royalty, the elaborate ceremonial and pageantry of state occasions, the splendor of the palaces, the gorgeous uniforms of the military men, the wit and beauty and finery of the women, all these things combined rapidly erased from her mind the little lessons learned from the Venerable Magdalen. All her strivings were now directed to one end — to become a second edition of the Montmorencys and the Guises and, for all her drawbacks, to cut as fine a figure as any of them. An envious rival might have described her as a colorless little creature with no looks to speak of, but Christine was keenly conscious of her good points: a dignified bearing, amiability, good intelligence, and an uncommon facility in expressing her thoughts.

With the tireless energy of youth she followed the never ending succession of entertainments organized by the various Court officials. Stag hunts were a favorite sport especially with the younger set and so she rode to hounds, but left to her own choice she preferred dancing to riding, persuaded that she performed much better in a ballroom than on horseback.

Her love of finery developed into a passion. Decked out in her mother's jewels and in garments, masterpieces of the dressmaker's art, she would spend hours admiring her reflection in a mirror. In fact, if sitting before a looking glass were the "infallible secret" of how to evolve into a beauty she ought to have turned out a Venus. However, as no magic results ensued she cheerfully decided to make the most of her intelligence and liked to be seen chatting with Corneille or some equally distinguished figure among the literary lions admitted to Court.

The favor that made her the envy of all her youthful contemporaries was the friendship of Anne-Marie-Louise de Montpensier, daughter of Gaston de Foix, Duke of Orleans, and niece of King Louis the Thirteenth. "Mademoiselle d'Epernon was my dearest friend," wrote La Grande Mademoiselle in her famous *Memoirs*. In the company of this beautiful and high-spirited girl, three years her junior, Christine attended balls and plays, concerts given by the royal orchestra of twenty-four violins and drives in the Cours-la-Reine. The two girls became inseparable. Once when a fit of piety took hold of Anne, Christine meekly joined in her devotions, listened to her reading the Life of St. Teresa, wore none but her plainest gowns to match Anne's "penitential" garb — and gaily dropped it all on her friend's return to normal.

Christine's distinction in the art of giving pleasure was acknowledged on all sides and her elders confirmed the opinion, generally held, that she inherited the more amiable of her royal grandfather's qualities: good nature, good humor, candor and readiness to trust others. No one who knew her — and she was the object of careful study on the part of the courtiers who could remember their beloved King Henry — no one who knew her could imagine her entertaining mean or suspicious thoughts about others. Blessed with a sweet mind she found it easy to be fond of people and to get on well with them. Compliments rained upon her; what wonder, then, that she was more than a little pleased with herself?

After her twentieth birthday her father decided the time had come to find a husband for her. His choice fell on a cousin of theirs, the Duke de Guise. She received this announcement with such lack of enthusiasm he immediately suspected her affections were already engaged. He was right. She was in love with a young officer, the Chevalier Charles de Fiesque, who, it was said, could look forward with confidence to a distinguished career in the army. Though her inferior in rank and fortune, he was her equal in every other respect. Upright and chivalrous by nature and utterly devoted to her, he was, she felt, the only man she would find it easy to love, honor, and obey. His family was descended from the House of Fieschi of Genoa which had given to the Church not only two popes, Innocent the Fourth (who approved the Carmelite Rule) and Adrian the Fifth, but also St. Catherine of Genoa, author of two highly esteemed works on the spiritual life: *The Dialogue of the Soul and the Body* and the *Treatise on Purgatory*. The Chevalier's grandfather had come to France as an official in the retinue of Queen Catherine de Medici and had made his home there. His mother, the Countess de Fiesque, was governess to Anne de Montpensier.

The young couple, though strongly attached to each other, were not formally betrothed when Charles was recalled to his regiment to go on active service. As he said good-bye to her, full of high hopes for their future together, he cheered her up with his boyish visions of military glory and success in the field. A week later the blow fell that put an end to these hopes: Charles was killed in the first engagement of the battle of Mardyck, 1646.

Months passed before Christine recovered from this shock. Her religion was her only consolation. However, in her days of mourning some memories of the recent past added more than a drop of bitterness to her cup of sorrow. One in particular. She remembered passing, on her way to visit a friend, through a large antechamber when suddenly her gaze had been caught and held by an immense picture on the wall depicting the "Ecce Homo." The blood-rimmed eyes seemed fixed on her, penetrating the depths of her soul, and at the same time she thought she heard these words spoken in her heart: "See what I have suffered for the love of you – and you, you never give Me a thought." Rooted to the spot, conscience-stricken, she had realized the justice of this reproach and had promised our Lord, there and then, to take up again the pious practices of her childhood. Her amendment of life had lasted three or four days. Too fond of a good time to be able to resist the appeal of legitimate pleasure, she had let herself be carried away in a whirl of gaiety, her pious resolutions not only broken but forgotten. On other occasions she had received similar, if less striking, reminders of God's unchanging love, such as impressions of His nearness to her, and of the attractiveness of a life with Him alone, but these, too, had proved equally ineffective. What these graces had failed to achieve within her when all was going well was now to be accomplished in a way she would never have dreamed of.

She was too much of a Bourbon to let herself sink into depression. With characteristic agreeableness she followed her stepmother's well-meant suggestions for her diversion and seemed to be almost her old self again. However, beneath this contented exterior there lay a strange uneasiness and a new seriousness. Gone forever were the days when, in her happy-go-lucky way, she could let tomorrow take care of itself. Now, on the contrary, whenever she found herself alone a question forced itself upon her attention which would not be silenced. What, it said, are you going to do with your life? You are twenty-two years of age. Your desire for marriage is dead and buried in Charles's grave. Quite apart from your wish to honor his memory, you neither hope nor wish to care for anyone else in the same way. Why not set your heart on God? Why not ask Him to teach you to love Him? This proposition made a strong appeal to her and she wished there was some friend with whom she could discuss it. To which the obvious answer was: the Carmelites. "Never," she said to herself. "I know well the advice they would give me, and I would rather be in my coffin than in a Carmelite convent." And she renewed her resolve to avoid them.

She was still in this unsettled frame of mind when one day a message came from the Queen inviting her to form part of her retinue on her visit on the feast of Our Lady of Mount Carmel to her old friends in the Faubourg St. Jacques. Christine would gladly have snatched at any excuse for absenting herself, but there was none. July 16 found her in her place in the royal suite as they were being ushered inside the enclosure door. While greetings were being exchanged she made straight for the choir, not with a desire to pray but simply to avoid meeting any of the nuns. She crossed over to the corner next to the tabernacle and had hardly got down on her knees when, in one flashing instant, she underwent a complete change of heart. She saw nothing, heard nothing, she only experienced this clear conviction: God wants me to give myself to Him in this holy house. She rose to her feet a changed being. Indecision, fear, repugnance were things of the past, and in their place came a deep, calm joy, and a purposefulness quite contrary to her natural character. She knew what was required of her and she wanted to do it, there and then. On leaving the choir she went in search of her stepmother, who had accompanied her to the Carmel, and, drawing her aside, told her what had happened. "So you understand," said Christine in conclusion, "that I cannot go home with you. I am staying here for good." The Duchess was struck speechless. She could not believe her ears. It seemed to her that Christine had taken leave of her senses. As soon as she could trust herself to speak she put this simple question to Christine: "What will your father say if I return without you? He will lay the blame on the nuns and then procure an ecclesiastical injunction compelling them to send you out of the convent. You cannot dispose of yourself without at least asking his permission." The Carmelites on their side, though overjoyed at this unhoped-for miracle of grace, lent their support to the Duchess' argument, and Christine, struck by the force of its logic, turned her steps homeward.

Fond as the Duchess was of Christine, she could not bring herself to be the one who should break the news to the Duke of his daughter's religious aspirations. After four years as the wife of Bernard, Duke of Epernon, she knew better than to broach in his presence any subject likely to incur his displeasure: Christine would have to do it herself.

Her heart quailed at the prospect. However, her love of God got the better of her fear of her father and, taking her courage in both hands, she knocked at the door of his study, advanced toward him, and poured out her whole story, omitting nothing. His first reaction was one of blank incredulity. Then, as she continued speaking, impressed by the impassioned earnestness of her manner, he realized he would have to take her seriously. By the time she had finished stating her case his self-control gave out, and pointing to the door he said in angry tones: "Don't you dare to mention that subject again. I absolutely forbid you to enter a convent. Mark my words, that so-called experience of yours was merely a figment of an overwrought imagination. You will forget it in a few weeks – and the sooner the better."

As the days and weeks succeeded one another he watched her closely and secretly marveled at the change that had taken place in her. Outwardly docile as ever, she nevertheless continued giving the same answer to the inquiries of her stepmother who had become their go-between: "I am convinced God wants me in Carmel and I am determined to go there." Her firm stand left him mystified. He knew Christine, he knew that far from being a strong, resolute character she was, on the contrary, too gentle, too yielding. Where had her newfound steadfastness come from? As with most men of his world, his religion was skin-deep. He knew next to nothing about the workings of divine grace nor was he interested in the matter. His one desire for his only daughter was a brilliant marriage and this he could easily arrange since there was not a young nobleman in France who would not consider it his crowning ambition to become son-in-law of the rich and powerful Duke of Epernon.

To cause her father pain and to see his affection for her cool overnight into positive hostility was no light ordeal for Christine. Adversity now brought into play, if not into being, qualities never before observed in her: constancy, thoughtfulness, sagacity. During this period she lost all her girlishness and became a woman — and a Christian through and through.

The Duke, exasperated by her inflexibility, ordered her to occupy herself in a manner becoming her rank: she was to accompany the Duchess on the social round and to maintain absolute silence on the subject of what she chose to call her Carmelite vocation.

Although she obeyed him to the letter, in the privacy of her own apartments she tried, self-directed, to lead a cloistered life. Well provided with *Lives* of the saints she devoured them eagerly and set about imitating their heroic example, especially in the matter of penance. With no spiritual director to lay a restraining hand on her fervors she carried penitential practices to extremes. For instance, social engagements permitting, she would, one day, fast on bread and water; another, cover herself with hair shirts and chains; and then again, if overflowing with spiritual consolations, she would spend the whole night in prayer. When the nuns in St. Jacques heard of these experiments, they felt they must warn her that in Carmel the practice of penance is intended to be not an end in itself but only a help in the life of prayer, "union with God," which is the vocation of a Carmelite; they then persuaded her to confine herself to making trial, as far as possible, of the life she hoped to lead in their company. If she were in Carmel, her day would begin in choir with an hour of mental prayer, followed by the recitation of the four Minor Hours of the Divine Office, then Holy Mass. After Thanksgiving she would leave choir and engage in the manual work assigned her until the sound of the convent bell would call her back to choir to make examen of conscience. Ten minutes later she would go for dinner to the refectory, where the rule of perpetual abstinence from meat and observance of Church fast for the greater part of the year allowed only a very simple meal to be served. Dinner and grace finished, there would be an hour's recreation, at the end of which she would continue her manual work. At 2 p.m. she would return to choir for Vespers after which she would do some spiritual reading in her cell until 3 p.m., when she would again occupy herself at household chores. Five o'clock would find her again in choir for another hour of mental prayer and at six o'clock she would go to the refectory for supper, or, from September 14 until Easter, for just a light collation. Another hour's recreation would follow and then she would return to choir to say Compline. Compline ended, she would have free time until 9 p.m. when the bell would summon her back to choir for the recitation of Matins and Lauds. A fifteen-minute examination of conscience would bring her day to a close and then she would go to her sparsely furnished cell to take her night's rest on a straw mattress. As Carmelite nuns live in strict enclosure she would never get a vacation of any kind nor would she be permitted to change from one Carmel to another.

She agreed to follow the wise advice of the nuns but unfortunately it came too late. Her penitential excesses had undermined her health with the result that she fell a ready victim to the epidemic of smallpox then raging in the city. A little later her father also took ill, and believing himself — or, more probably, pretending — to be in danger of death, summoned Christine to his side. Submissive as always, she made her way, with assistance, to his room. With an air of great solemnity he informed her of the purpose of his summons: he was about to make his will; if she promised him to abandon all thought of entering religion he, on his side, would divide his possessions equally between herself and her brother; if not, Jean would be his sole heir. Christine made no pretense of reflecting on the matter. Without the slightest hesitation she gave him her answer: "I am sorry to have to displease you but I cannot make that promise."

Weeks later when both of them were convalescing together the Duke devised a new stratagem for breaking down her resistance. This time he centered his efforts on the most vulnerable part of her nature, her affectionate heart. In their long talks together they came very close to each other and he assured her repeatedly that she did not know how much she meant to him. His only daughter, she was the apple of his eye, how could she think of leaving him? Nothing could make up to him for her absence, the thought of losing her was unbearable, and many more protestations in the same vein. This approach was the one most likely to carry the day. Never before had he spoken to her in language so tender, so affecting. To stand firm, unyielding in the face of this moving revelation of her father's deep affection for her, cost her some moments of intense anguish, yet there was no temptation to give in. In a letter written a few days later to an intimate friend she described her feelings in these words: "My heart is by no means insensitive; yet at this moment where family affections are concerned it is as hard as a rock. I simply could not prefer them, any of my relatives, to God. You know what a weakling I have always been; at present, however, I feel so changed, so full of strength that, dearly though I love my relations, to leave them will not cost me a tear. If it is God's will that I must never again lay eyes on any of them, I shall not hesitate to obey Him. From now on, my only interest in life is to please God."

Her restoration to health was much retarded by her realization of the futility of trying to gain her father's consent to her entrance into religion. The Duke made a supreme effort to persuade Christine that though a Carmelite vocation might be a good thing for the ordinary run of girls, for her, a princess of the blood, it was a piece of insanity. After bringing forward many arguments in support of his contention, he ended by an earnest appeal to her native good sense: "If only you would leave your future in my hands you would soon be happily married to a man of your own rank."

A wholly unforeseen circumstance presently favored the Duke's design. At this very time Ladislaus the Fourth, King of Poland, wrote to Queen Anne to inform her that as his wife, Maria of Gonzaga, was childless and had no hope of bearing an heir, he wanted to secure the succession to the Crown to his brother, Prince Casimir. Now, in order to safeguard the execution of his plan he wished the Prince to marry into one or other of the great families of France and so obtain French support of his claim. The good-natured Queen, more than pleased to have an opportunity of trying her hand at matchmaking, took careful stock of all the unmarried girls at Court to decide which one of them seemed best fitted to become the future Queen of Poland. Her close scrutiny found all the qualities required in only one of them, Christine. In a confidential letter to the Duke of Epernon she passed on this information, complimenting him on having a daughter who would do honor to both France and Poland. The Duke's gratification was only equaled by his amazement at this providential intervention in his daughter's affairs. Son-in-law of a king, he reveled in the thought of becoming father of a queen and congratulated himself on his opposition to his daughter's religious projects. He immediately wrote to her Majesty, expressing his gratitude for her condescension to his family and his readiness to sign the marriage contract without delay.

The first intimation received by Christine of her betrothal to Prince Casimir came *after* the contract had been signed and was on its way to Warsaw for ratification by King Ladislaus. The announcement filled her with despair. As the arrangement had originated with Queen Anne of Austria it amounted to a royal command; there was no way of evading it.

Ever since that visit to the Carmelites on Mount Carmel Day, Christine had been kept under supervision by her parents. With increasing disquiet they observed the devout life she was leading, her frequent attendance at church services, her patent reluctance to appear at Court, and both were agreed that the only way to inveigle her into marriage was to keep her in the dark until the last moment. When all the arrangements had been made to his complete satisfaction, the Duke informed Christine that the signal honor bestowed on her by the Queen indicated her Majesty's affectionate concern for her happiness and that the Duke of Arpajon, as ambassador extraordinary entrusted with the negotiations, was already en route to Warsaw to bring them to a happy conclusion; King Ladislaus' signature would give them binding force and it would be obtained in little more than two months. The date of the wedding was for her to fix. The marriage portion he had settled on her was ample, even by royal standards. He went on to assure her that, as the future Queen of Poland, she could look forward to a life full of opportunities of serving not only God and His Church in that troubled country but also her brother's interests. Cardinal Mazarin, who had a finger in this matrimonial pie, had taken Jean under his patronage; consequently the young Duke, if brother-in-law of Prince Casimir, could aspire to the highest offices in the land. Christine, though not very shrewd, saw through her father's device for forcing her consent by appealing to her two great loves: Jesus Christ and her brother. With the utmost deference she begged him not to deceive himself with the hope of this brilliant alliance; she had given her heart to Jesus Christ and she trusted Him to deliver her from any earthly espousals. The Duke pretended not to have heard her words but warned her that, being his child, she was bound to obey him, willingly or unwillingly; and then saying: "I expect you to behave like a sensible girl and fall in line with my wishes," he left her to herself.

The horror with which she shrank from the prospect of her approaching marriage affected her so seriously that it brought on an attack of shingles. No sooner had she regained a little strength than her doctor prescribed a course of the waters of Bourbon. Her father, profoundly perturbed at her altered appearance, urged her to complete the cure of the waters by a long rest at their castle in Guyenne.

Christine readily agreed to comply with these instructions, perceiving that they afforded a way of escape, even if but a temporary one, from the seeming fate in store for her. Then the unexpected happened. On the day fixed for her departure for Guyenne, Paris was ringing with the latest news from Poland: King Ladislaus was dead. He had passed away shortly before the arrival in Warsaw of the Duke of Arpajon. She was free.

Her lost vitality returned overnight. Realizing that if she was to take advantage of this unlooked-for situation, she would have to act quickly, she set to work to make a complete break with the world. Her plan was simple: she would enter the first Carmelite convent lying on her route southward; this would be the one at Bourges. With Mother Agnes de Bellefonds for her accomplice she made arrangements with the Bourges community to receive her – temporarily – when, in a few days, she would knock at their door.

Chapter 3

The visible improvement in Christine's health and looks on the day she was due to leave Paris did not escape her father's notice. In case she might see in King Ladislaus' death a divine intervention in her favor the Duke let her know he had no intention of abandoning his matrimonial designs for her; quite the reverse. Whereupon Christine reminded him, respectfully but firmly, that he ought to remember she had never budged an inch from her decision to refuse all proposals of marriage. This undiplomatic rejoinder was more than he could take. He treated her to a lecture on the spirit of disobedience and obstinacy by which, he said, she was still possessed: she was forgetting she was still under his authority, from which no priest could exempt her. Both of them then proceeded to bring in the Bible in support of their respective contentions, the father quoting texts from the Old Testament extolling the blessings promised to children who honor their parents, the daughter contenting herself with repeating the most appropriate text from the New Testament: "He that will have father or mother before Me is not worthy of Me." Feeling out of his depth in scriptural quotation, the Duke directed the conversation into safer and calmer channels and then left her, hoping that a few months traveling through the extensive family estates in Guyenne would bring Christine to a reasonable frame of mind.

September 6, 1648, dawned with every promise of pleasant weather for a journey by road. The sun had not climbed high in the sky when Christine in the company of the Duchess and a numerous retinue set out on the first lap of the long drive to Bourges. Charmed by all they could see from the carriage windows of the pretty countryside and of the interesting villages where they halted for a change of horses, they reached Bourges before sunset. The next day was spent there, resting; and Christine, with the wisdom of the evangelical serpent, never left her stepmother's side. The Duchess, not having the least suspicion of what was afoot, never dreamed of keeping a watch on her stepdaughter's movements. Counting on this absence of supervision, Christine rose early the following morning and, attended by two of her maids of honor who, unknown to all, shared her determination to join the Carmelites of Bourges, sent for the carriage to take them to the convent. The nuns fully informed of every detail of her plan, were waiting in readiness at the enclosure door. No sooner had the carriage stopped than the three young ladies, breathless with excitement, hurriedly alighted and almost ran to the door, which immediately swung open to admit them. They were in Carmel. Christine could not speak for joy. Her two years of struggle and hope deferred were at an end. A happy smile lit up her face as she laid aside her fashionable clothes and put on the plain brown habit of the daughters of St. Teresa.

In less than an hour the servants who had escorted Christine on her early morning drive, having seen her and her maids of honor enter the Carmelite enclosure, hastened back to the Duchess with their alarming report. At first she refused to believe that meek and mild Christine could have had the hardihood to take so bold a step without a word to anyone, but when at length she realized that the girl had indeed given her the slip, her anger terrified the bystanders. Jumping into the carriage, she drove pell-mell to the convent, ordered the Prioress to bring Christine to her at once, and at sight of her beloved stepdaughter dressed in the Carmelite habit her self-control broke down completely. Fixing the brand-new novice with a baleful glare she stormed and raged, using dire threats one minute and fair promises the next in the hope of getting her out of the convent under any pretext. At last she commanded her, in the name of the Duke, to return home with her on the spot. Christine tried in vain to reason with her. The Duchess, full of dismay at the thought of having to bring such tidings to her husband, at last tore herself away from the Carmel and ordered the coachman to drive back to Paris.

To say that Christine's religious elopement took her father by surprise is an understatement; it dealt him the most unexpected blow of his life. When his wrath had quieted down sufficiently to allow him to collect his thoughts he wrote her this letter:

My child,

The blessing of God cannot follow you in the life you have chosen for yourself. How could it, since you have broken the Divine Law as expressed in the Fourth Commandment: "Honor thy father"? You have not honored me. On the contrary, you have flouted my wishes and ignored my rights. Being underage you are under my authority and cannot dispose of yourself in opposition to my known wishes. I demand your immediate return to your family.

What makes you think that a featherheaded, pleasure-loving girl, such as you have always shown yourself to be, can persevere in a monastic Order of strict observance? And how will your health stand the strain of such a life since in even the most favorable conditions it succumbed to every kind of fever?

I promise you I will move heaven and earth to get you out of that convent. This is no empty threat. As you know, I have highly placed friends in both Church and State who can have you dispensed from your vows and removed from your cloister, removed by main force, if necessary.

If you persist in your disobedience you shall be to me as one dead. More, I will lay my curse upon you, you rebellious, contemptuous child.

Unless you change your mind and return home this very day I shut you out forever from my heart and from my thoughts. I never again want to hear from you or of you. Do not send letters to me; I will not read them.

Come home at once: this is final. This is the last letter you will ever get from

Your greatly offended
Father.

If a letter could have constrained her to abandon her vocation this is the only one that could have succeeded.

Cut to the heart by its tone and contents, she read it in tears; for she loved her father dearly, and the harsh contrast between the tender intimacy during their convalescence together and the cold cruelty of this ultimatum left her a prey to mournful reflections. But not for one moment did her resolution waver. At a loss to know what measures to take to soften her father's obduracy and bring him around eventually to see her point of view so that they might become father and daughter to each other again, she wondered if an appeal to the Queen would serve this purpose. Sure of her Majesty's sincere affection for her, as well as of her willingness to do her a service, more especially one in furtherance of God's interests, Christine poured her heart out in a letter to Queen Anne. To her deep disappointment the Queen ignored her appeal. What Christine did not know was that at that particular time Cardinal Mazarin, the Prime Minister, was finding the Duke of Epernon a first-rate henchman in the prosecution of State affairs and consequently urged her Majesty to refrain from intervening in the Duke's domestic difficulties.

Actually, Duke Bernard was far from being the heartless tyrant his letter makes him appear. Throughout the three long years of his hostility to Christine he secretly engaged the services of discreet persons to obtain for him at regular intervals truthful answers to these three questions. First, was her health keeping up? Second, was her resolution showing any signs of weakening? Third, was there any likelihood of the nuns inducing her to leave out of fear of incurring the enmity of the Duke's influential friends? Had he known the members of that community he would never have entertained the hope of intimidating them. They were mettlesome noblewomen, all of whom had had to fight their way into the convent against parents and relatives who accused them of wishing to commit a strange kind of suicide – exchanging a splendid life at Court for a miserable existence in a large tomb. And these nuns had a stock answer for visitors who condoled with them on their loss of social standing: "With the King of Heaven for our Bridegroom, the Creator of the universe for our Father, and the Holy Spirit for our intimate Friend, we live and move in the Highest Society."

Immediately after her entrance into Carmel Christine wished to show her love of all whom she had left by giving each of them a keepsake. To her father she sent a beautiful portrait of her mother (the Duchess Gabrielle) and her Book of Hours; to her stepmother, a ring and two diamond bracelets with the request that she would wear them in memory of her; and to every member of the household, from the first gentleman-in-waiting to the last of the domestics, a present that was sure to give them pleasure. The family retainers had always been attached to her, but never more so than when they saw her renounce, with an air of sweetness, all the things that youth holds dear.

Two days later she took her departure from Bourges and set out for Paris accompanied by Mother Agnes de Bellefonds of the Carmel of the Faubourg St. Jacques into which she made formal entrance, September 10, 1648.

This was the celebrated Monastery of the Incarnation, founded in 1604 to receive the first Discalced Carmelites ever to set foot on French soil. They were led by the Venerable Anne of Jesus, and her five companions were almost her equals in social distinction and in reputation for saintliness of life. This Carmel differed greatly from St. Joseph's, Avila (the cradle of the Reform). Built to the specifications of Madame Barbe Acarie (known now as Blessed Mary of the Incarnation) and at the expense of the royal ladies interested in the project, it stood at the corner of the Rue de St. Jacques and the Rue d'Enfer, an imposing building containing forty-eight cells in addition to the usual monastic offices. The ornamentation of the chapel was on a grandiose scale, the frescoes having been painted under the personal direction of Phillippe de Champagne, prince of French painters. Christine was not impressed by this splendor. In later life when asked for her opinion of some new decorations she replied: "The aspect of a Carmelite chapel should be conducive to converse with God rather than to admiration of works of art."

Shortly after her arrival at this Carmel, came a visit from her brother Jean, Duke of Candale. Just turned twenty-one years of age, he was numbered among the coming men at the Court of the Queen Regent, Anne of Austria; yet his family feeling was stronger than his personal ambition. This was proved by the sincerity and disinterestedness of his love for Christine: her refusal of Prince Casimir's hand, with the consequent loss of prestige to himself, did not in any way alter his affection for her. His first impression of a Carmelite parlor was far from favorable. On seeing his darling sister separated from him by a double grille he wept unrestrainedly. As soon as he got his voice under control he launched out, without preamble, on the subject of her retirement from the world, following up the attack where their stepmother had left off. Christine heard him out in silence, entreating all the saints in heaven to help him see her point of view. Then looking at him with the humorous smile he knew so well, she asked: "Do you think the future King of Poland would want me, now that I have my hair docked?" That remark having brought a touch of comic relief into the conversation, she went on to tell him of all that had happened to her since their last meeting and, finally, asked him if he liked her new name: Sister Anne-Marie of Jesus.

When, after a conversation lasting more than two hours, he took leave of her, he was fonder of her than ever before and promised to support her cause with their father.

Some days later she was again called to the parlor, this time to give an account of herself to the Queen, who came accompanied by Queen Henrietta of England (aunt of Christine), the Princess de Condé (mother of the Great Condé), and the Duke of Orleans (uncle of Christine). Anne of Austria, whose deep affection for and interest in Christine was so deep that she had been accustomed to speak of her as "my niece," or "my daughter," now greeted her with marked coldness. Forgetting the letter Christine had sent her the very day of her entrance, she heaped reproaches upon her, accusing her of having ignored the rights of authority by taking the law into her own hands and running away from the world without leave or license from anybody. Though at first disturbed by this severity, Christine quickly recovered herself and with her gift of ready speech soon convinced the Queen of the genuineness and imperiousness of her call, and in a very short time their intercourse was on its former friendly footing. Before leaving, the two royal ladies, as well as the Princess de Condé and the Duke of Orleans, gave Christine their word that they would write to her father in the hope of persuading him to readmit her to his good graces.

The promises were kept, but all to no purpose. Duke Bernard was down in Guyenne rendering valuable services in that distracted province. The four letters only hardened him in his resolve to disown Christine for good unless she gave in to his wishes. Scarcely a month earlier he had succeeded in extracting a promise from Cardinal Mazarin to use his influence with the ecclesiastical authorities in Rome to issue a papal summons ordering the Lady Christine d'Epernon to return to her family. At her visit, Queen Anne had confided to Christine that formal application for this summons was under consideration at the moment but that the Cardinal, having business of the gravest description on hand and anxious to win the good will of the Vatican, was loath to sign his name to such a petition.

Throughout her first three years in the convent Sister Anne-Marie lived in daily dread of being forcibly removed from it. Strange to say, her strength, both physical and moral, proved equal to the strain. Prompted by the Prioress and instructed by learned priests she composed a memorial to be sent to the Holy See for the purpose of obtaining for herself its express permission to make her profession as a Carmelite nun. In due time came the hoped-for letter granting her request with full approval; more, Pope Innocent the Tenth sent her not only his blessing but also his personal congratulations on her choice of the religious state.

The day of her profession, September 21, 1650, which saw the crowning of all her hopes, was a joyful occasion not merely for herself and the community but for her intimate friends. These, few in number but of tried loyalty, came to the Carmel to congratulate her in person. So moved were they at the sight of her transparent happiness that they urged her to write to her father inviting him to visit her now that she had become a bride of Christ. "If only he could see you he would certainly relent," they told her. Taking up their suggestion with enthusiasm she set to work with pen and paper and poured out her joy in words that ought, she felt, to melt a stone. One of the friends offered to take the letter to him. On recognizing the handwriting the Duke refused to touch it. "Take it back to her," he said, "and remind her that I have forbidden her to have any communication with me."

Chapter 4

It was not difficult for the Duke of Epernon to dismiss his daughter from his thoughts. He was, at this particular time, enjoying the spectacular success of his administration in the peculiarly harassing situation in Guyenne where Frenchmen had been fighting Frenchmen for what each side sincerely believed to be the good of France.

After the death of Richelieu the Duke's talents found full scope and he acquitted himself brilliantly in his duties as military commander and governor of Guyenne. Fully aware of his abilities and his services, he looked forward confidently to adequate acknowledgement from his friend, Cardinal Mazarin, and he was not disappointed. Recognition came to him in its most acceptable form — promotion; he was advanced from the governorship of Guyenne to that of Burgundy. His successor in Guyenne was the Prince de Condé.

One day shortly after he had taken up his new appointment he happened to be passing through a village situated about a mile or so distant from Clairvaux. As the fine weather made traveling a pleasure he decided to visit the tomb of his patron, St. Bernard. On arrival at the historic abbey he was received with due honor and conducted to the shrine containing the relics of the Founder of the Cistercians. The tranquil atmosphere of that celebrated house of prayer had its effect on him. Charmed by its contrast to the bustling activity in which he spent his days, he forgot his cares of state and took a genuine interest in all that was laid out for his inspection. Last of all he was shown the Saint's scapular. Quite unaccountably he was taken with a sudden impulse to put it on. So great a favor could not be refused the Governor of Burgundy. The Abbot asked him to kneel, and the Duke obeyed. No sooner had the scapular rested on his shoulders than these words, in some mysterious way, were impressed upon his mind: "Your daughter has chosen the better part which shall never be taken away from her." At the same time, he saw, in a flash, what manner of man he himself was, and the part that he had chosen for himself. For several minutes he remained on his knees, stunned by this revelation. He left the abbey a changed man and completed his journey in profound agitation.

Dazed by this strange experience his thoughts were slow in returning to their normal orderliness, and as soon as he felt equal to the business of letter writing his first care was to send to Christine a full account of his change of heart.

His letter began with a request for her blessing in return for his curse and went on to tell of the light in which he now saw himself. He saw himself to be a sinner, his life a heaving mass of sin. Sins of pride – how he had exulted in his own success and despised his rivals in their failure! Sins of injustice, of vindictiveness, of weakness – such was the state he had lived in. An unscrupulous conscience had allowed him to possess the peace enjoyed by men of ill will; he had never given a thought to the moral consequences of his actions. Far from forgiving his enemies, he had always hardened his heart against them and returned evil for evil, as opportunity offered. Henceforward, he assured her, all would be different. At present his one wish was to be, and to remain,

God's good friend, and to undo all his misdeeds as far as lay in his power.

What weighed most heavily on his newly awakened conscience, he told her, was the recollection of his campaign during the civil war when he had laid exorbitant exactions on certain townsfolk and had permitted his troops to pillage to their hearts' content. Already, he added, his most trustworthy agent was on his way to that town with instructions to inquire into the amount of damage done and to make restitution on the most liberal scale to all having any claim to compensation.

His letter ended with a touching appeal. Now that he had made up his mind to devote the remainder of his life to the work of his salvation he called on her to help him on his way by acting as his spiritual guide. When Sister Anne-Marie folded his letter it was blotted all over with the happiest tears she had ever shed in her life.

On his return to Paris his first visit was to the Carmel. A new relationship sprang up between them, much more tender, much more intimate than any they had ever known before, he her humble disciple, she his humble tutor. He came to her frequently for consultation on the affairs of his soul. She began by recommending him to put first things first, illustrating this counsel by an experience of her own. One day, about ten years earlier, she had been starting on a journey through his estates in Guyenne when she suddenly remembered it was August 20, feast of St. Bernard, her father's name day. She immediately ordered the coachman to drive her to the nearest church where she could hear Mass and receive the Eucharist. On entering she was dismayed to find that it was in a dilapidated condition, and when the priest faced the congregation to distribute Holy Communion she was shocked to see that the ciborium was a small wooden box with a badly fitting lid. Her thanksgiving finished, she made straight for the sacristy and, to the priest's surprise, pressed her purse into his hand, asking him to provide a proper tabernacle and ciborium. The Duke was horror-stricken at this story and promised to inspect all the churches on his property for the purpose of making ample provision for all their requirements.

On his own initiative he resolved to set right all the injustices of which he was guilty and did so, promptly and conscientiously. As he asked her for any further suggestions she thought well to make, she reminded him of the importance attached to almsgiving in both the Old and New Testaments. He forthwith made arrangements for regular distribution of immense sums of money among destitute persons, especially those living on his own estates.

These first duties having been attended to, he took his first steps in the interior life. At his request, Sister Anne-Marie became his teacher in the art of cultivating the friendship of God and she illustrated her lessons with detailed descriptions of her own mistakes in making mental prayer.

As far as was practicable he shared in her life as a Carmelite and, like a fervent novice, took her instructions to heart and regulated his life by Christian principles.

Like the two good children of God that they were, father and daughter never ceased to marvel at the great mercy He had shown them; it was their favorite topic of conversation. Both of them recipients of the rare grace of transformation, instantaneous, irresistible, efficacious, they took their responsibilities seriously and encouraged each other to live up to the teaching of the Gospel.

The deeper Duke Bernard entered into the life of prayer the better he realized how inimical to it is the bustle of the great world. To Christine's intense joy he confided to her his decision to withdraw from it as well as from Court circles. He also told her of his intention of resigning from all those high offices he had acquired at the cost of infinite pains and clever maneuvering. More, he would henceforward lead a simple life, that is, simple by comparison with the standard of his fellow peers, and, far from Paris with its rivalries and intrigues, spend the years that were left to him in thinking of God and the things of God.

From this time on Duke Bernard and Sister Anne-Marie communicated with each other by letter, and this correspondence became the one unfailing joy of the remaining years of his life. His desire for the sanctities of a life of prayer was stimulated by passages from her letters such as this one: "My love for our Lord is now so deep that I cannot imagine how it can ever become deeper. His life is my life. I relive in spirit His mysteries as the commemoration of each one of them comes around each year. Now that Easter is here I am consumed with the longing to lead a risen life, the life that Jesus won for you and me on the first Easter Day."

From his very first week of solitude and silence he began to improve his acquaintance with the person he had scarcely known until that turning point in his life on his visit to Clairvaux Abbey, the person that was his hidden, real self. On that unforgettable occasion a ray of divine light had given him a moment of piercing self-knowledge, a touch of Purgatory. In the intervening months he had been so fully occupied settling his affairs in accordance with his daughter's suggestions – providing dowries for portionless aspirants to the religious life, establishing schools and hospitals throughout his estates, as well as arranging for the preaching of continual missions there – that there had been no time for him either to have a leisurely look at himself or to take stock of his spiritual accounts. Too sincere merely to play at being a Carthusian, he took the rough edge of solitude along with the smooth and let it do its work unhindered by pleasing distractions.

His first experience took formidable shape, the revival of an old temptation of his, hatred of his enemies. With nothing to divert his thoughts into safer channels he suffered torments from its violence. From morning until night his mind seethed with bitter recollections of the harm he had suffered at their hands. Old grudges reappeared and became obsessions. The conviction grew in him that he never had forgiven and never could forgive injuries. In deep dismay he wrote to ask his daughter if he would not be better occupied in the government of the province of Burgundy than in the contemplation of his soul so full of evil passions.

In order to deal with her father's difficulties Sister Anne-Marie must have enlisted the help of the Prioress, Mother Agnes de Bellefonds. Broad hints of the advisability of his seeking guidance from a priest were firmly ignored. Duke Bernard, having met too many Richelieus and Mazarins, had more confidence in his daughter's advice than in that of any priest; in his opinion she had this impressive advantage over the eminent clerics of the day – she was all out for God.

In a long letter packed with texts from Scripture she initiated him into the Church's time-honored teaching of the superiority of the will over the sensibility. No one, no matter how spiritual he may be, is in complete control of his feelings, whereas he is always sole master of his will. Obviously, then, all her father had to do was to pray for the strength of will always to reject those feelings, never to entertain them voluntarily. Furthermore, should they beset him for days or weeks on end, he must not lose courage; God was bound to come to his aid and help him to keep on resisting. Then, with the utmost delicacy, she asked him if he could not bring himself to see in this temptation an opportunity of expiating the sins whereby he himself had provoked hatred in the hearts of his unsuccessful rivals. Lastly, she reminded him that temptations of this sort, besides bringing the sufferer the inestimable benefit of experimental knowledge of his utter dependence on God, supply him with occasions for exercising spiritual valor.

Intelligent and reasonable and wholehearted in pursuing his new way of life, the Duke understood the sound advice given in the letter and pondered over its concluding words: "Keep in mind what St. Paul implied when he wrote in his Epistle to the Romans* that all of us were at one time His enemies.

Turned wholly to God and favored occasionally with glimpses of His divine charm, Duke Bernard gradually lost all interest in the world that had formerly meant everything to him, and living as a sort of hermit, became a contemplative in his way. On his rare visits to Paris, made only when strictly necessary, whatever time he could spare from interviews with his men of business was spent with his daughter. He loved to listen to her speak of prayer. She told him that the mystery of the Incarnation was the usual subject of her meditations and that the Blessed Eucharist was the chief source of her consolations. Then, knowing of his difficulties, she taught him from her own experience how to cope with distractions, distaste and beginners' impatience with the slowness of God's leading. The secret of success here, as at every other stage of the quest for God, is to be found in that text from the Epistle to the Hebrews which says in effect: "Fix your eyes on Jesus."** This must be done as much as one can, but, emphatically, without imposing any strain on the mind. And though intimacy with God is the pearl of great price, it is not bought at the cost of strenuous mental effort: "prayer consists

* Cf. 5:10.
** Cf. 12:2.

in loving much rather than in thinking much."

Careful to keep his mind nourished with the best of spiritual reading, she urged him to go through the New Testament meditatively, and later on she introduced him to the works of her holy mother, St. Teresa, and other religious classics. He was moved to hear her say that she did not understand why certain preachers spoke of the world with scorn. For her part, she never tired of repeating this verse in St. John's Gospel: "God so loved the world that he gave his only-begotten Son that whosoever believes in him may not perish but may have life everlasting." She, too, loved the world and interceded for it with God and felt nothing but compassion for the great sufferings that are the lot of so many persons living in it.

Sister Anne-Marie did something more than converse in the parlor on Carmelite life with God; she made this life a daily reality. The verse of Psalm 83: "I have chosen to be the last in the house of my God," she adopted as her device and put into practice. In her concern to be no different from the rest of the community she took her turn at all the rough work, scrubbing the kitchen floor and tables, washing clothes, as well as doing her full share of the lighter household chores, such as sweeping, dusting, etc. Doubtless, her lack of efficiency made her more of a hindrance than a help, but her goodwill and good humor endeared her to the Sisters to whom she was assistant so that they hated having to correct her. If any of them tried to spare her a messy job she would say playfully: "Stop thief, you are robbing me of my merit!" In all her fifty-three years of religious life the only office to which she was elected, and that only once, was the office of bursar.

From her very entrance into the cloister she was visited by all her old friends who found, to their delight, that by exchanging stylish attire for the Carmelite habit she had lost none of her charm. Her dramatic withdrawal from the world had made her the heroine of the hour, and they wished to see for themselves how she was faring in the austere convent she had chosen for herself. From the first she made it clear that gossip held no interest for her, they accordingly left the direction of the conversation to her and so she talked of what was nearest her heart, the love of Jesus Christ. She spoke of Him as simply and unaffectedly as if He was a dearly loved friend she expected to see in a day or two. Her visitors were enchanted. Not all of them, however. Her youthful friends, including Anne de Montpensier (who had poured scorn on her religious aspirations) found her preachy and starchy. In her famous *Memoirs* Anne wrote: "During the two hours I spent with her, Mademoiselle d'Epernon scolded me so severely I did nothing but weep." Exasperated by their tiresome expostulations at her strange choice and annoyed by Anne's championing of the rebel faction (under the leadership of the Great Condé), Sister Anne-Marie cared little what impression she made on them.

Though by nature a captivating talker she became in time an understanding listener. Serious-minded people felt drawn to her, sensing in her the sincerity and womanly feeling they expected to find in a true spouse of Christ. Her heart went out instinctively to sufferers of all kinds, especially to those who had met with sudden reverses of fortune. Their need of sympathy and assistance was her opportunity. Throughout the years of the civil wars several persons of rank and wealth found themselves disgraced and impoverished overnight. Many of them were directed to the Carmel of the Faubourg St. Jacques where consolation came to them in confiding their troubles to Sister Anne-Marie. And not merely consolation. A widowed noblewoman who had made known to her her financial difficulties received from Queen Anne of Austria, at Sister Anne-Marie's request, an annual pension of seven hundred écus, and, after the Queen's death, regular payment of it continued, again at Sister Anne-Marie's request, by Anne de Montpensier, during the remaining twenty-seven years of the widow's life.

This instance — only one of many — is typical of the part Sister Anne-Marie was to play throughout her long life in Carmel: enormous sums of money passed through her hands in relief of hidden poverty. It is also typical of her other and higher role, the one proper to a Carmelite, that of mediator between God and sinners. Just as she had used her influence with her royal cousins to obtain material help, and even pardon, for political unfortunates, so also she exercised her rights as a spouse of Christ to get supernatural life and divine forgiveness for mortal enemies of God.

No one benefited more largely by her prayers than did her uncle, Gaston de Foix, Duke of Orleans. Everybody knows he was one of the most despicable men ever heard of; his vices are matter of history; not one redeeming trait absolves his character from the charge of utter baseness. Though well aware that his infamies were no secret from his Carmelite niece, he, for some obscure reason known only to himself, became one of her regular callers. At the end of his visits he invariably asked if there was anything he could do for her, to which she invariably replied: "Give me an alms for God's poor so that it may draw down His mercy on you." This occasional almsgiving was, possibly, the only good use this gambler ever made of money.

On hearing, in 1659, the grave news of his stroke (from which, however, he made a rapid and apparently complete recovery), she redoubled her prayers that he would make a Christian death, vain though such a hope seemed at the time. In her eleven years in Carmel, frequent and profound meditation on the Passion of Christ had brought home to her this one of its many lessons, that inborn baseness — surely the most mysterious element in the mystery of evil — is to be treated by the mature Christian not with the contempt and hostility it deserves but rather with the understanding and assistance it needs. Understanding: "There go I, but for the grace of God; my own good qualities are not of my own making." Assistance: prayer (backed up by sacrifice) to our God who can draw good out of evil and transform scarlet sinfulness into snow-white innocence. At her uncle's last visits, she dropped her former attitude of disapproval and, on the contrary, treated him with the same considerateness as would Jesus Christ were He in her place. Gaston's response to this new approach surpassed her highest hopes. Though feeling in the best of health and with no presentiment of his rapidly approaching death, he seemed to be touched by her affectionate concern for his spiritual welfare and promised her to take life seriously. She eventually worked him around to the point where he agreed to think over the four last things: death, judgment, heaven, hell. With this first big step in the right direction his vices began to lose their grip on him. Who among those that had known him at any period of his life would ever have dreamed that, at fifty-one years of age, Gaston of Orleans (who had betrayed all his best friends to the scaffold and swindled his own daughter out of half her property) would spend his last six months on earth in one long sustained effort to bring the affairs of his soul into some semblance of order?

Though Sister Anne-Marie was the first princess of the blood to enter the Carmelite Order, she only ranks among its lesser luminaries. No spiritual genius of even the most modest description, she had neither doctrine to pass on to others nor mission to accomplish in the Church at large or within the narrow confines of her own Order. Her sole claim to memory lies in the signal success attending her intercession for sinners. Doubtless, the secret of this success lay in the power she had gained over our Lord's heart by making His Sermon on the Mount her rule of life. In that sublime discourse Sister Anne-Marie of Jesus had found a self-portrait of her Spouse, Jesus, the divine Exemplar of its counsels, the unique Possessor of its beatitudes. The more frequently she read it the more clearly she understood that, if only she modeled her life on it, she could hope to become a living likeness of Jesus, a helpmate like to Him, bearing not only His name but also His image; then God, the Father, looking on her, would say: "This is My beloved child in whom I am well pleased." And she wondered if therein lay the explanation of that obscure saying of our Lord: "If you ask the Father anything in my name, I will do it."*

* Jn 14:13.

Chapter 5

At her brother's first visit to her in Carmel Sister Anne-Marie had extracted from him the promise to do all in his power to gain a just hearing of her cause from their father, and Jean, on his side, had asked her to pray for him every day of her life.

He needed these prayers. A handsome, lively young man, he had sown his wild oats in dashing style but without in any way compromising his chances of advancement: at thirty years of age he had become Viceroy of Catalonia (at that time a French possession). In reply to her anxious inquiries concerning his faith he assured her he believed whatever was taught by the One True Church, the only trouble being his inconsistency in not living up to his beliefs. However, she found consolation in the thought that he never left a kind deed undone. For example, once when riding along a country road he caught sight of a man lying bruised and bleeding in the ditch, obviously the victim of a carriage accident. Instantly dismounting he picked up the injured man, put him on his horse, and supporting him with an arm walked beside him until they reached a village. Here he had him comfortably lodged in the best inn and gave the landlord a substantial sum of money to cover the expenses. On his return journey some weeks later he called at the inn to ask after the invalid, who ran up to him, completely recovered from his injuries and loudly expressing his gratitude to his good Samaritan.

In 1658 Jean's prospects were at their brightest when, quite unaccountably, he was struck down by a fatal illness. He had just left Paris where he had bidden Sister Anne-Marie an affectionate farewell after a long and serious talk with her in the course of which he had told her he carried out his duties to the best of his ability. For instance, he had put a stop to dueling among the soldiers and officials under his authority, visited them in time of sickness and in case of necessity asked the chaplain to give them the consolations of religion. On arrival at Lyons he began to feel slightly unwell. By the following day he had developed alarming symptoms, severe pain and high fever. His secretary immediately notified Sister Anne-Marie who at once wrote to a friend of hers residing at Lyons with the request to visit him and prepare him for death. "I know my brother intimately," she said. "Perhaps he is no worse, certainly he is no better, than his associates. I have always thought that he takes much too lighthearted a view of his sins; he does not see them as offenses against God. Try to get him to make a thoroughly sincere preparation for confession and ask him to accept death with his will, regardless of his natural repugnance. But above all things, impress on him the greatness of God's love for him. Choose your words carefully lest he should fall into despair and if he shows any tendency in this direction speak to him earnestly of the infinite mercy of God, stressing the point that to despair of the divine goodness is to commit the saddest sin of all."

Although grief-stricken at the thought of her own loss, she entreated heaven for only one blessing, the grace of a happy death for Jean.

A week later came a letter from her friend describing the last days and death of the young Duke. After the first attack of acute pain he understood from the doctor's hints that he had been poisoned. The full horror of death seized upon him, paralyzing his faculties. He could not think, could not pray. All he knew was that hateful pain and hateful death were his inescapable lot. How he wished that Christine could come to him! Several days passed before her friend visited his sickroom and by that time his spirit of faith was beginning to revive so that he welcomed the suggestion to make his peace with God. The memory of his sinful life afflicted him grievously and she heard him often say in a voice broken with sobs: "What would I not give to be able to get back the wasted years so that I might use them well!" He tried his best to bear his suffering in a spirit of atonement. Once when he thought he was alone she heard him utter these words in heart-rending accents: "O Lord God, make my heart sincerely humble and contrite so that I may know Thou wilt not reject me – which, in truth, is what I deserve." Having confessed all the sins of his life he summoned his servants and domestics to his presence. As soon as all had assembled in the sickroom he began his short deathbed speech. First, he asked pardon for all the bad example he had given them, and then having thanked them for their loyal service he concluded with a truly heroic act. Calling up his last remaining strength he made this declaration: "With my last breath I wish to say – and I wish I could say it in public – that I ask forgiveness of my enemies for all the harm I have done them and I, in my turn, forgive them for all the harm they have done me." The priest then administered the Last Sacraments and after a devout thanksgiving the dying man again asked pardon for all the scandal he had given, adding: "When I think of all the evil I have done, I only wish I had a few more years of life in which to do penance." A few minutes later he gave his soul back to God.

To his last will and testament he made this addition: "To my darling sister Christine I leave my heart in token of the love and gratitude I bear her, asking that it may be buried in her convent chapel where she will pray for me as long as she lives."

Sister Anne-Marie mourned Jean's death with such abundance of tears that for two months she got hardly any sleep, yet her sorrow was much sweetened by recollecting the grace of perfect contrition with which he had been favored.

For her father there was no such consolation. If Jean had died from natural causes he might have accepted his loss with Christian resignation, but the thought that his only son – his sole heir upon whom all his hopes were centered – had been cut off in the flower of his age by the hand of an assassin brought his contemplative life to an abrupt end. The poison that had brought the young Duke to an early grave seemed to have passed into the heart of the old Duke, with lamentable consequences. His old temptation, hatred of his enemies, flared up again, this time with redoubled violence. Once more he felt incapable of saying this petition of the Our Father, "Forgive us our trespasses, as we forgive those who trespass against us."

In the few lines he sent his daughter he made no secret of his near despair. He had given up praying and taken to brooding; he never could grant pardon to the murderer of his son, nor could he endure the idea that the House of Epernon had come to an end.

Much more grieved by the effects of Jean's death on her father than by the tragedy itself, Sister Anne-Marie called on Mother Agnes' assistance to compose a letter which might help to deliver him from this grave temptation as well as from his utter dejection. It opened with carefully worded sentences in which she let him know how fully she shared his sense of loss and how her sadness was mingled with holy pride at the memory of Jean's words of pardon on his deathbed. Then she put this question to him:

> I wonder if you can take this view of Jean's untimely end. You know, and Jesus Christ knows, that at one time you were an enemy of His; yet He has forgiven and forgotten all. Can you bring yourself to see in the present tragic occurrence an opportunity for you to pay to Jesus Christ the debt of forgiveness you owe Him? You are a resolute character: to make a decision comes easy to you; why not make this one? You can do it in the strength of Christ who has commanded us not only to pardon our enemies, but even to love them. This divine commandment is not impossible of fulfillment. We can pray for the strength to sincerely wish to fulfill it, and who knows but that He may accept the will for the deed?
>
> As for your lament that the House of Epernon is to become extinct, won't it bring you some drop of consolation to reflect that it is going to die out in a spouse of Christ? True, our name will be forgotten in the annals of the world, but what does that matter? You and I know it is written in the Book of Life.

Duke Bernard never got over the shock of Jean's death. It aged him sadly and although eventually his spiritual forces rallied, his physical powers steadily declined. Communication with the convent became his sole support. Under the influence of the wise advice and tactful sympathy contained in letters from the Carmel he gradually lost interest in everything except his friendship with God. In this frame of mind he turned easily to reflections on the transitoriness of all earthly things, sorrows no less than joys, and visits to his daughter became the one bright spot in his otherwise cheerless existence. Even when infirmity had reduced him to a condition of helplessness he had himself carried into the convent parlor, and together father and child talked of the invisible world toward which he was rapidly advancing.

At what they both knew to be their last meeting he was overcome with emotion. His eyes glistening with tears, he addressed her in these words: "My dear, good daughter, I cannot describe my gratitude to you except by saying that you have been to me what St. Monica was to St. Augustine; keep me always in your prayers." He went on then to thank her from his heart for all the affection she had lavished on him and for her forgiveness of things for which he could never forgive himself. In a voice broken with emotion he called on God to send down His best blessing on this beloved child, the sole joy of his declining years. Then bowing his head he asked her to bless him and so they said a last good-bye to each other with many tears.

A few weeks later Duke Bernard died. In the last letters to Sister Anne-Marie written at his dictation he said that, peaceful and free from all care, he was again enjoying the consoling presence of God, that his days were filled with prayer and that he was looking forward to meeting Him face to face. Shortly after (in 1661) Sister Anne-Marie received the news of his death: it had been as holy and as happy as even she could have wished. The few words that fell from his dying lips expressed nothing but boundless confidence in the mercy of God. And his last request was: "Ask Christine to send me her blessing."

Chapter 6

The last surviving member of her family, Sister Anne-Marie understood in a new way the meaning of St. Teresa's favorite maxim: God alone. To fathom its depths was to be the occupation of the many long years she would pass in Carmel. After the first frightening sense of loneliness had passed away she recognized each day more clearly her indebtedness to God for the uncovenanted mercies He had poured out so bountifully on her father, her brother, and herself and her inability to render Him adequate thanks. Henceforth all the sinners in the world would be her concern as if they were her own kith and kin and she would spend herself to win for them the friendship of God and the means to preserve it.

To live the Carmelite life to the full had been her ideal from her novitiate, and the passage of time brought no lowering of her standards. A fellow religious said of her: "If by any misfortune the spirit of fervor in our monastery should diminish, Sister Anne-Marie's example alone would restore it." That this impression was not due to blind admiration the following incidents will show. After her brother's death, her father often made immense gifts to the community, in addition to the annuity of eight hundred écus he had settled on her. Though not at all shrewd, she divined the consequences –

preferential treatment, etc. – likely to follow and accordingly took steps to offset any moves in this direction. When the Prioress (Mother Agnes) one day recommended having her threadbare habit replaced by a new one, Sister Anne-Marie would not hear of such a suggestion. "Oh, please Mother," she protested, "leave me the one I am wearing. I honestly like this patched habit." And in the height of summer when the Prioress, noticing her air of exhaustion, would say: "Let me get you a habit of lighter material," she would again object: "I beg of you, let me wear the same kind of habit as do the other Sisters." If the Prioress suggested her taking extra food or extra sleep she was sure to beg off with: "Believe me, Mother, I was born to keep the Carmelite Rule, for truly I never feel better than when I am observing it without any dispensation."

Not many years after her entrance into religion Sister Anne-Marie discovered that all the leading members of the community performed extra penances and made extra vigils so, of course, she thought she ought to do the same. If the Prioress had not known how to curb her enthusiasms she would have gone to extremes in these matters.

Never to complain seems to have been one of the resolutions she kept most faithfully. It happened that once she was given, by mistake, an undergarment of new serge which had not been washed. The feel of the material told her this; nevertheless without a word to anyone she put it on. At the end of a week her skin was so severely chafed that the pain robbed her of sleep for almost three months. This was not an isolated incident; it was typical of her observance of the Carmelite Rule. By way of explanation she said she was glad to find such opportunities of expiating the fastidious excesses of her youth.

Needless to say she had difficulties to contend with. Given

her pleasant and pleasure-loving disposition, the monotony of cloistered life must have palled on her many and many a time but she never made a song about it. Her gay and sunny nature together with her resilient spirits was a great boon to herself and to everyone in the convent. The mere sight of her brought to mind St. Paul's dictum that God loves a cheerful giver and encouraged the other Sisters to go and do likewise. Up against pretty much the same difficulties as Sister Anne-Marie, they could guess at the pressure she put on herself to keep smiling all the time.

Blessed by nature with the desire to please, she naturally experienced the drawbacks it carries with it. Every year she had to make the same resolution: "I must try to please *God alone,* not other people, not myself." If by a miracle she had been able to live up to that high ideal she would not have been upset at being misunderstood, at unrequited cordiality, at lack of appreciation. Her most conspicuous fault was a tendency to put a fair face on her little mistakes. For example, at the ceremony solemnizing the burial of her brother's heart in the Carmel she was overcome by an uncontrollable fit of weeping so that her sobs drowned the voices of the praying nuns. As soon as she regained her composure she was all concern to remove the impression she might have given of being attached to Jean and unresigned to the will of God. And certainly she did her Sisters less than justice if she feared to lose their regard because her grief got the better of her self-control.

Traces of touchiness could be seen in her now and then. If her visitors happened, no matter how innocently, to remind her of the levities of her salad days she would change the subject of conversation with an air of displeasure as much as to say: "I want to forget all that." And once when her uncle, Gaston of Orleans, being in a playful mood teased her about her former enjoyment of Court functions, especially those of a more diverting nature, she said to him: "I thank God every day of my life for taking me away from that dung-hill."

Her social gifts, which in worldly company had been her chief asset, became in community life an occasion of meritorious self-restraint. How often she would have liked to talk at the times when silence was imposed by the Rule! And how sorely she was tempted to confine her attention to the attractive members of the community and to avoid the Sisters of forbidding aspect! Her failure in these tests brought her many a correction and these she accepted with sincere humility.

Whether she was serving her week in the kitchen or in the laundry there was one duty from which she was never exempt, that of entertaining the royal ladies at their visits to the parlor or to the interior of the convent. For more than one reason this duty must have caused her serious inconvenience but her compassion for the secret sorrows of several members of the royal family made her only too happy to be able to bring them the consolation and encouragement they stood in need of. In particular her aunt, Queen Henrietta (daughter of Henry the Fourth of France and widow of Charles the First of England) who never forgot that the Duke of Epernon when living in London had lent her husband the enormous sum of six hundred thousand livres *and* had, later on, canceled the debt.

An equally illustrious visitor came in the person of the consort of Louis the Fourteenth. While Louise, Duchess de la Valliere reigned for ten years as the virtual Queen of France, the real Queen, Marie Therese (daughter of the King of Spain) came frequently to find solace and privacy in the hermitage she had had built for herself in the monastery garden. Here, safe from prying eyes and from the ill-natured pity of the courtiers, she felt at ease and, to quote her own words, could breathe again the air of her native land, conversing in Spanish with the daughters of a Spanish mother, the Carmelite reformer, St. Teresa of Avila.

Other callers of less exalted rank included the Prince de Conti and his sister, the Princess de Longueville, both of whom always maintained that they owed their reconciliation to the Church to their friendship with Sister Anne-Marie. Convinced Jansenists at their first meeting with her in Carmel, they were more conscious of the objections to Catholicism than of its attractions. She did not set out to convert them; being much cleverer than her they could have worsted her in any argument. What won them over was the impression of sheer goodness that emanated from her; in her they thought they could see the truth and beauty of the One True Church. Accustomed to the austere airs assumed by the nuns of Port Royal they found Sister Anne-Marie a study in contrast – simple, unassuming, human in the best sense of the word.

The practice of humility presented her with little difficulty. Throughout her life the memory of the sensational circumstances attending her entrance to Carmel lived on in the great world and brought on her a steady stream of adulation from queens and princesses as well as the open admiration of spiritual connoisseurs such as Bishop Bossuet and the Superiors of the French Carmel; yet all this esteem caused her not a shadow of vainglory. It would seem that her first grace of conversion carried with it the realization that in answering the call to Carmel she was only an unprofitable servant doing what she was obliged to do.

Another point of assistance to Sister Anne-Marie in maintaining a humble opinion of herself was the distinction of the community with whom she lived. Its foundress was Blessed

Mary of the Incarnation; after her came the Venerable Magdalen of St. Joseph, intimate friend and disciple of de Berulle,* and then a succession of prioresses who, one could well believe from reading their biographies, were in every respect the equals of St. Teresa's "circle of great prioresses" to quote Marcelle Auclair's useful phrase.

Let us take a look at just two of these nuns, beginning with Sister Anne-Marie's novice mistress, Mother Agnes, in the world Judith de Bellefond. She was born in 1611 in her family's ancestral home, the castle at Caen, and grew into an attractive child, so attractive that at the age of twelve she was taken to Paris — much against the wishes of her sincerely devout mother — by her aunt, the wife of Marshal de Geran. This lady had Judith presented at Court and, gratified at the favorable impression made by the child, soon busied herself with matrimonial speculations and plans for the benefit of her niece. Though serious-minded by nature and sensibly brought up by her mother, Judith had no defenses against the flatteries lavished on her appearance, her amiability, and other pleasing qualities. In no time the wise warnings of her mother were forgotten and the seductive charm of Court life had made another captive. After five or six years of this delightful existence the ease with which her mind had turned to God was replaced by a certain constraint, yet in the midst of the gayest entertainments the still small voice of conscience sometimes made itself heard in her heart with ever the same reminder: "You were born for something more worthwhile than these empty pleasures." And even though she enjoyed them she would have no peace of mind until she had renewed her childhood's promise to God to give herself to Him in the cloister. The sincerity of these renewals stood up to the test

* Peter Cardinal de Berulle, founder of the French Oratory and author of some religious classics.

of her aunt's indefatigable matchmaking; Judith never lent herself to any of the Maréchale's schemes.

An occasion not of her own choosing was to light her path to the house where God wished her to make her home with Him. This was the Carmel de Paris where a cousin of her mother's, the Marchioness de Bréaute, was professed under the name Sister Mary of Jesus. Judith's day of destiny came when a message from the Queen (Marie de Medici) ordered her to take her place among the maids of honor in attendance on her Majesty at a ceremony in the Carmelite convent. On arriving at the chapel the young girl was directed to sit between the Papal Nuncio and Cardinal de Berulle. During the ceremony a lady seated behind Judith kept on questioning her about the ritual as well as other religious matters. The Cardinal was so struck by the good sense of her answers combined with the modesty of her bearing that he besought God earnestly to call her to the Order of Carmel. His prayer, together with that of the nuns whose intercession he had enlisted, was heard. Despite the opposition of all her family, her mother alone excepted, she made arrangements to enter the convent and fixed the day for January 20, 1629. At the last minute on the evening of the nineteenth she was assailed by a fierce temptation to back out. A horror of the cloister swept over her. To enter it seemed a mad act; nevertheless at the height of the storm that raged in her breast she betook herself to prayer. The following morning, dead against her natural inclinations but armed with divine fortitude, she forced herself into the convent. She was eighteen years of age.

With the Venerable Magdalen for her novice mistress she learned how to combat temptations.

Two months after her entrance she received the holy habit and her new name, Agnes of Jesus.

One year later she made her profession. On this occasion

also she suffered a violent temptation against her vocation. Far from feeling all aglow with holy joy at the privilege of being officially espoused to Jesus Christ, she was overwhelmed with a sense of loathing of Carmelite life. Each of the conventual exercises seemed so intolerably burdensome, she felt she could not push herself through another day of it. Again the great Novice Mistress came to the rescue, this time aiding and heartening her with the texts of Scripture helpful to a religious in the grip of this particular snare.

Sister Agnes was going through an apprenticeship that was to turn her into a valiant woman. Infirmarian to the Venerable Magdalen during the last eight years of that holy nun's life when, a martyr to severe pain of body and soul, the great Carmelite reproduced some modest likeness of Jesus crucified, the young nun got a training of the most impressive kind. At nineteen years of age, witness of pure suffering borne with sublime patience, she learned the secret of the unique work it accomplishes, interior resemblance to Jesus Christ, and at the end of the eight years asked Him – doubtless under divine inspiration – for the grace of suffering well.

Perhaps it was in answer to this petition that within a few weeks, eye trouble developed, causing her such pain that total blindness was feared. Though only twenty-seven years old, calm and resigned she set herself to learn the Psalter by heart, so that she would always be able to recite the Breviary. However, contrary to the doctor's expectations the disease cleared up and her sight continued unimpaired.

Thirteen years later she was elected Prioress. Endowed with every quality required for governing well, she won the undying affection of her community, who entrusted her with offices of authority as long as she lived.

The chief characteristic of Sister Agnes of Jesus, uprightness, can be seen to advantage in these few incidents. After the death of a woman friend of hers who had made the Carmelites her sole legatees, it was found that the lady was liable for a number of debts. Immediately after this fact came to Mother Agnes' knowledge she not only waived all claim to the inheritance but got together the costly Church ornaments presented from time to time by the deceased lady, had them valued, then sold and had the proceeds forwarded anonymously to the rightful heirs. Another friend of hers, the Duchess de Guise, once asked her as a favor to be allowed to enter the enclosure, at the same time offering the princely alms of one hundred thousand livres. Graciously refusing it she explained that as this privilege was reserved for members of the royal family alone, she had no power to extend it to anyone else. And even when the visits of the queens with their retinues became too frequent she did not hesitate to beg them to come less often, to which request the royal ladies readily acceded.

In quality of benefactress Charlotte Marguerite de Montmorency, Princess de Condé (mother of the Grand Condé) enjoyed the privilege of residing at certain seasons within the cloister. When she asked Mother Agnes if this favor extended to her personal maid, the Prioress was not afraid to cause the great lady deep disappointment by a firm refusal. And one day as the Duchess de Guise was thanking her profusely for permission to talk to the community, she dryly replied: "I don't know if people gain anything from visits with Carmelites, but I do know that it is the nuns who stand to lose."

She had a flair for – of all things – jurisprudence. Adept at elucidating the knottiest points of ecclesiastical discipline she enjoyed the reputation of being something of an expert in Canon Law. Furthermore, she mastered the Rules and Constitutions of all the Orders in the Church – an accomplishment that was of service to those of her priest friends actively engaged in the religious revival of seventeenth-century France. It must be added in parenthesis that the de Bellefonds were not a legal family. Judith's father like almost every other nobleman in France took part in the wars of his day, and both her uncle and nephew were marshals of France.

From the time when as a young nun Mother Agnes had nursed the Venerable Magdalen, her resolve to lead a crucified life had never faltered. In her ardor for the Cross she found the austerities of Carmel insufficient. To these she added such penances as extra disciplines, the hair shirt, and restricting herself to three or four hours' rest, which she took on a plank bed. Not content with eating less food than the allotted portion she rendered that little unpalatable by mixing with it some bitter herbs. The motive of this penitential life was, in part at least, atonement for the scandalous life of the Merry Monarch, whose salvation had been entrusted to her personally by his mother.

After the flight of the royal Stuarts from England, Queen Henrietta became one of the regular visitors to the Faubourg St. Jacques. On a few occasions she insisted on her two little sons accompanying her into the interior of the Carmel in the hope that close contact with high sanctity would change these young Protestants into good Catholics. While thirteen-year-old Charles would fidget on his chair, the picture of sullenness bordering on open rebellion, James seemed to be almost enjoying the strangeness of his surroundings. Stanch little Anglican that he was, he met the nun's objections to his branch of Christianity with intelligent answers and, though only a child, showed a taste for religious controversy. Moved to see so young a boy attached to his religion and so loyal in defending it, Sister Agnes looked on him and loved him and needed no entreaties from his mother to take him under her wing. She contented herself with making this pact with him: "If you promise me to ask God every day of your life to show you which of the two is the One True Church, I on my side promise to make this same petition on your behalf." Fifty years later, a dethroned monarch, he renewed his friendship with the Carmelites. At his visits he loved to remind his "guardian angel" of this conversation, saying it had often come back to him in memory with a vividness he could not account for. And he assured the community that he attributed to their intercession the deathbed conversion of his brother.

Mother Agnes' harshness was directed against only one person – herself. To others, as has been seen with Sister Anne-Marie, she showed the tenderness and even the indulgence of a mother. To the begging fraternity who thronged the convent side door she was a fairy godmother. Not only did she give them alms in abundance, she was lavish with something they valued more; when any of the women among them asked the Portress if they could have a talk with Reverend Mother they never got a refusal. Her sincere love of the poor made her blind to their faults and compassionate to their sufferings. Indeed she was never more herself than when listening to her beggar-women friends pouring out their woes. And it was to their intercession she attributed her recovery from a fatal illness.

No more than the rest of mortals she did not escape ill-natured criticism. Her community being composed mainly of aristocrats they were accused of worldliness, haughtiness, etc. True to her high ideals, she bore in mind that the only effective answer to slander is the one recommended in the evangelical counsels. There is no evidence of her ever having read the works of St. John of the Cross, but she had his spirit. Where there was no love she put love and found love.

Such was Mother Agnes of Jesus who, as novice mistress, introduced Sister Anne-Marie to Carmelite life. Now let us meet another great nun under whose authority Sister Anne-Marie lived for a number of years, namely, Mother Marie Madeleine de Bains.

Although at some points the vocation of Marie Lancri de Bains followed pretty much the same pattern as that of Judith de Bellefonds, the two girls themselves had, in some respects, more marks of difference than of resemblance. Acclaimed on all sides as the most beautiful girl at the Court of Henry the Third, Marie was besieged with suitors, to each of whom she said no. Her proud and doting mother, full of matrimonial plans on her behalf, could not rest until she had wrung from her the secret of her reluctance to marry. In fear and trembling Marie confessed that at each of her visits to the Carmel in the Faubourg St. Jacques, to which, being maid-of-honor to the Queen, she had frequent access, she felt an irresistible attraction to the way of life led there and an unshakable conviction that God was calling her to it. Madame de Bains was completely unprepared for such an avowal. But, as soon as she regained her power of speech, she expressed her feelings with unladylike candor, and not only to her daughter but to everyone within earshot. All the courtiers joined with her in scouting the very idea of Marie having such a vocation and leagued themselves together against its accomplishment. Meanwhile a good portrait of her had found its way into the convent and as it was being handed around at recreation each of the nuns put up the same petition: "All-powerful God, please call this lovely young girl to our Carmel." Sister Mary of St. Teresa, daughter of Blessed Mary of the Incarnation (Barbe Acarie), took the matter so much to heart that she there and then offered herself to God to suffer whatever He might require in return for such a favor. Finally, at the age of twenty, after two years of heroic resistance to appeals and threats, the fair Marie succeeded in battling her way into the cloister. In a last-minute effort to hold her back, her mother waylaid her in the convent garden and for three hours pleaded, argued, wept, raged until, exhausted and defeated, she took her departure, leaving Marie worn out but in undisputed possession of the field.

The Novice Mistress subjected Marie's vocation to a singular test. For several weeks after her entry Marie was obliged to meet in the parlor those of her faithful swains who called, the most persistent of whom being the Duke de Bellegarde and the Marshal de St. Luc. As she continued saying no to all of them, the Novice Mistress declared herself satisfied with the genuineness of her vocation and gave her the holy habit.

Shortly after her Clothing, feeling sure of her ground, the fervent novice tracked down the much-admired portrait and burned it.

When little more than ten years in the convent, she was elected prioress. In addition to beauty, charm, and practical intelligence she was gifted with a rare personality, magnetic as well as persuasive. Throughout her many years in authority she exercised such an ascendancy over her spiritual daughters that after her death one of them paid her this amazing tribute: "If she told us black was white, or day was night we would have believed her unhesitatingly; we held her to be infallible."

During the civil wars her affectionate heart suffered much from its attachment on one side to Queen Anne of Austria and on the other to the Princess de Longueville (sister of the Grand Condé) both of whom were intimate friends of hers as well as generous benefactors of the Order. More distressing still were the alarms and excursions affecting her community. One evening when all were at prayer in choir, word came that the rebels had marked down the convent for burning that very night. Bombshell though this message was, she kept her head and in a very short time completed arrangements for the Sisters' safety. The older nuns to the number of seventeen she dispatched to the Carmel of Pontoise in carriages lent by the Princess, while she herself and the juniors, including Sister Anne-Marie, took refuge nearer home in the Carmel of the Rue Chapon. At the time she did not know that the message was but a false alarm and that both the community and the convent would escape harm.

In the biographical sketches of each of Sister Anne-Marie's contemporaries in the Carmel de Paris a negative point worthy of note is the silence concerning extraordinary mystical phenomena of every description. The terms used by Saint Teresa to indicate the various states of prayer and the corresponding favors are never even alluded to. This is probably due to the posthumous influence of Blessed Mary (Acarie) who, it will be remembered, at her first reading of St. Teresa's *Life* was put off by the frequent mention of visions, ecstasies, etc., and became quite skeptical of the objective reality of such marvels.

As might be expected in a milieu characterized by the sober spirituality of the New Testament and of St. Teresa's "Way of Perfection" petty devotions were frowned upon. The most eminent preachers in Paris willingly accepted invitations to give sermons to the Carmelites, knowing that in this community they had an audience who not only appreciated their finest flights of oratory but also understood their teaching and put it into practice.

Bossuet preached his Lenten conferences in their chapel in the year 1661, and from that time on exercised considerable influence on the community. He passed on to them his own passion for the Bible. It was from listening to his oral commentaries that Sister Anne-Marie advanced in understanding of Scripture. On his advice she read the Bible through at least once a year. In the course of her long life she became so familiar with both the Old and the New Testaments as to merit the tribute paid by St. Jerome to a disciple of his: "By her diligent reading and her long meditations she made her heart the library of Christ." Naturally it was to the New Testament she turned to find the object of her search: the whole truth about Jesus Christ. She pored over the Gospels, finding in them – the only authentic *Life* of Christ – the living portrait of Him whom she desired to love, honor, and obey with her whole heart. By studying His instructions, His ways, His preferences she learned how to please and charm Him so that He would be glad and not sorry to have asked her to share her life with Him. Loving meditative reading of these pages showed her the mind of Christ and pondering over His words and actions she came to see what were the qualities that won His highest praise, what the defects that incurred His most frequent rebuke. Again and again she resolved to be a woman of great faith, one who could see – and love Him – beneath His most impenetrable disguise, the neighbor with whom she rubbed shoulders.

The Psalter was her favorite book of the Old Testament. Bossuet's conferences opened up for her the hidden beauty of this, the greatest book of poetry of all time. In time she gained an insight into the currents and undercurrents of its meaning and learned by heart those of the psalms in harmony with the vicissitudes of life. When the sky of her small world was overcast she would find relief in repeating the psalms expressive of hope of better times to come; then again when all was bathed in sunshine the opening verses of Psalm 103 would rise to her lips: "Bless the Lord, my soul; O Lord my God, what magnificence is thine! Glory and beauty are thy clothing. The light is a garment thou dost wrap about thee, the heavens a curtain thy hand unfolds. . . ." Long familiarity with the psalms perfected her taste for God, *vera sapientia.* Given the period, the convent library was well stocked with religious books of all kinds but the older she grew the less she cared for them; the Bible alone met all the needs of her soul, the Psalter being her prayer book. The only poems that are truly of divine inspiration could not fail to awaken in a heart emptied of self-occupation a longing to know their Author. She formed the habit of saying the psalms in union with Jesus and Mary, thinking with joy of the fervor with which they sang: "Come praise the Lord all you that are the Lord's servants; you that wait on the Lord's house at midnight lift up your hands towards the sanctuary and bless the Lord. May the Lord who dwells in Sion bless thee, the Lord who made heaven and earth" (Ps 133).

Choral recitation of the Divine Office was for her, as one would expect, an unfailing source of consolation. The thought of the long procession of saints who had sung their hearts out to God in the greatest love lyrics of all time made her yearn to join her poor treble to theirs in the hope of catching some spark of their spirit. With this idea in mind she read her Breviary with love and joy regardless of her feelings of fatigue, of cold, or irritation at the faulty pronunciation proceeding from some nearby choir stall. In the great psalms of Blessing she found an outlet for the gratitude that welled up in her heart for the glorious gift of life, life with its inexhaustible possibilities of loving. She wanted to love God as did the saints who had given voice to their grand passion in the identical words before her in the Breviary.

Appreciative of the gift of life, she had no heart in chanting this verse of the Canticle of Ezechiah: "I will recount to thee all my years in the bitterness of my soul." No, the long vista of her seventy-seven years of life appeared to be flowing with milk and honey, and she found comfort in reciting one or other of the psalms that render thanks for the divine bounty. How differently she would have used those precious years had not God intervened and taken her "out of the swing of the sea"! In review she could see the greatest benefit brought her by life in the cloister was the gift of knowledge. *Illuminabit abscondita tenebrarum et manifestabit Se.* – "He will bring to light the things hidden in darkness and will unveil Himself." For her, as for every true contemplative, the life of prayer consisted in a steady progress in the knowledge of truth – the truth about God, Infinite Holiness personified, and the truth about herself, human wretchedness incarnate. The descent into the depths of her heart revealed such misery as would have plunged her in despair but for the firm and experienced hand of Mother Agnes who steered her safely through the deeps and shoals of that most treacherous passage of her spiritual voyage. *Et manifestabit Se.* Having let her see what she was in herself, God then unveiled before her humbled eyes something of His divine charm, not in the flashing splendors bestowed on a St. Teresa but dimly, in the awareness of His presence, and this awareness kept on increasing imperceptibly until it became the atmosphere in which she lived. And more than once, after receiving Holy Communion, she was favored with the sublime experience of understanding in some degree the love of God that is in Christ Jesus our Lord.

Like every good Catholic she went to Jesus through Mary, and like every good nun she had her favorite saints: hers, in order of preference were St. Joseph, St. Teresa, St. Mary Magdalen, and St. Augustine.

Owing to the enlightened instruction given her as a novice there was nothing vague or soft in her devotion to our Lady. Tenderness there was but no sentimentality. It was based on the only direction given by the Mother of Christ recorded in the Gospel: "Do whatever He tells you." The miracle that rewarded the obedience of the servants at Cana was to be worked for her, too; the paltry human love that was all she was capable of would, in the course of her lifetime, be turned into the ardor that makes saints. And so she took Mary for her model. To see Jesus through Mary's eyes, to love Him with her heart — that is to adore Him as God, to follow His example in all things, to hearken to His counsels and thus become, like both Jesus and Mary, a true child of God the Father — that was the simple Mariology taught and practiced in the Carmel de Paris.

Chapter 7

The years slipped by, each one like the last, with nothing to vary the rhythm of the chief festivals in the Carmelite almanac. Christmas, *the* great day in the Monastery of the Incarnation was followed by the Epiphany. Then came Easter, *the* great day in Sister Anne-Marie's calendar as well as in that of the Church. Each year the joy and wonder of the Resurrection came back to her with the freshness of a paradisal spring and St. Paul's text: "seeking the things that are above, we are risen with Christ" set her mind straining to catch a glimpse of the human-divine reality behind it. Last of all came Pentecost. She loved to let her mind dwell on the scene described in the Acts of the Apostles: Mary presiding over the group of the first Christians gathered together in seclusion and in prayerful expectation of the "Promised One of the Father," and then the mighty Spirit of God swooping down on each one of them, transforming the group of weaklings into a band of heroes eager to do and dare all for the love of Jesus Christ.

In Sister Anne-Marie's uneventful life there was nothing to vary the rhythm of the feasts commemorating the chief mysteries of our Lord's life, nothing except echoes from the troubled world outside and from the other convents of the French Carmel. The Order was still attracting vocations in ever mounting numbers from every class of society, from every age group. During her lifetime the Reform of St. Teresa spread so widely that before the celebration of its centenary in 1662 every large town in France had its Carmel. And Sister Anne-Marie cannot have failed to hear with interest of the founding of several houses of Carmelite nuns in Poland, where her unknown and unloved fiancé of the distant past was now King Casimir.

Domestic events marked dates that later served as points of reference. One of these was unforgettable. Not long after the marriage of King Louis (aged 48) to Madame de Maintenon (aged 50), the King came to the convent to pay his respects to the community and afterward gave them a talk, a sort of conference.

Another, and earlier, event, still more memorable, was the entrance into Carmel of Louise, Duchess de la Valliere. Since she and Sister Anne-Marie were not only fellow religious for twenty-six years but also had connections by marriage (Louise's daughter Marianne becoming the wife of the Prince de Conti) a short sketch of the famous penitent may not be an unpardonable digression.

Louise Françoise de la Baume le Blanc de la Valliere was born in 1644 of one of the great families of Touraine. Her father, the Governor of Amboise, dying early and her mother remarrying, Louise was brought up in the family of Gaston, Duke of Orleans. After his death she became, at the age of sixteen, maid of honor to the youthful Duchess Henrietta (daughter of Queen Henrietta of England and wife of Philip, Gaston's nephew and successor to the duchy of Orleans).

With masses of golden hair framing her lovely face, Louise adorned whatever company she found herself in. She would have been quite perfect but for one serious drawback, she had little of the attic wit and conversational brilliance so highly prized by her contemporaries. Her education had not been of the best and neither was her intelligence, nevertheless on appearing at Court she was an immediate success. What drew people to her was not so much her looks – there were prettier girls galore in Versailles – as the strong suggestion of pathos in her large blue eyes shining with innocence, trustfulness, shyness – qualities quite rare in that artificial world. The admiration and flattery heaped upon her seemed to glance off her simple heart, leaving it completely unaffected. Then came the fatal day when, at seventeen years of age in the full glory of her girlish attractiveness, she caught the roving eye of the twenty-three-year-old Louis the Fourteenth. The first moment their eyes met she fell passionately in love with him, and for the next eleven years the most splendid court known to history lay at her feet. Little did she care for its splendors; all her solicitude was to please the King (to her he was a demigod rather than a man) and to mind the children she bore him. Of these, only two survived childhood: the girl Marianne, born in 1666 whom she always addressed as Mademoiselle de Blois, while the little one on her side called her, "my beautiful Mummy"; the boy, Louis, born in 1667, was named the Duke de Vermandois.

The King legitimatized both children and created Louise, Duchess de Vaujour. This honor, far from making her feel elated, only cast her into the depths of shame; to her mind it was the wages of her sin. She never called herself de Vaujour. Furthermore, even during those years when her infatuation with Louis was at its most indecent, she never neglected her religious duties; on the contrary she practiced them as far as was compatible with the immoral life she was leading. And she never refused an appeal for alms. One day, as she was going out for a drive in her carriage, she was accosted by a beggar asking a little help for the love of God. The Duchess instantly opened her purse and offered him a handful of gold pieces. Dumbfounded by such largess the poor man gazed at her for some moments in silence and then said: "Ah, lady, you are sure to be saved. No one who gives so generously to the poor for the love of God could be lost."

For eleven years she reigned in the pleasure palace of Versailles, the envy of many an unsuccessful rival, the despair of her few true friends. To no one did she confide the torturing disquietude in her soul. Qualms of conscience within, strong denunciations without – the eloquent tongues of both Bourdaloue and Bossuet scourged the vices of that corrupt Court – nothing had the power to subdue the passion that enslaved her to her demigod.

However, in 1670, the sudden death of her friend, the nineteen-year-old Duchess Henrietta of Orleans, put the fear of God into her and so, without a word to anyone, she ran away to the Visitation Convent in Chaillot with the intention of breaking with her life of sin. As soon as Louis got to know of her whereabouts he sent messengers to the convent to bring her back to him by force. Shortly after, she made a second attempt at hiding herself among the Visitandines in the same convent, but with the same result. To prevent her from playing any more tricks of this kind on him, the King heaped on her the tenderest reproaches and from then on put forth all his powers of fascination to keep her in his toils. His efforts met with perfect success.

The passing of a very few years brought a change. With the arrival of Madame de Montespan on the scene, Louise was eclipsed. Seeing herself now ignored by the King just as his lawful wife Queen Marie Therese had been ignored when she herself had been in the ascendant, Louise went through the twofold agony of rejected love and remorse of conscience. With nothing to hinder her now from attending to the affairs of her soul, she saw that her first duty was to do penance for her sins and, on reflection, she decided to expiate them in the very place where she had committed them, the palace of Versailles. Ample opportunity of doing so was provided by her supplanter, Madame de Montespan. As Louise remained on in the suite of rooms formerly assigned for her use, the two young ladies met every day. The haughty beauty went out of her way to pour scorn and ridicule on the unfortunate Louise who, in her turn, accepted it as just punishment for the scandal she had given. The courtiers looking on ascribed her meekness to want of spirit and applauded the biting sarcasms heaped upon her by the King's new favorite.

Now that Louise was free to enter on a life of penance in the cloister, a serious difficulty presented itself: what was to become of her children? She loved them devotedly, especially Marianne, then a charming child of twelve and passionately attached to her mother. Her friend, Marshal de Bellefonds (nephew of Mother Agnes), having introduced her to Bossuet, she laid all her perplexities before him, but he, already acquainted with her affairs through the Marshal, encouraged her to make her own decisions. After some talks with Mother Agnes and Sister Anne-Marie, Louise felt certain it was to the Order of Carmel our Lord was calling her. Mindful of His unequivocal statement, "He that prefers father or mother or children to Me is not worthy of Me," she knew the painful duty that was hers to perform. The following extract from a letter written by her at this time shows how far she had advanced in understanding the life of sacrifice that stretched before her: "Great as is my affection for my children it is not great enough to make me turn a deaf ear to the voice of God urging me to do penance for the sins I committed in bringing them into the world." And further on: "It is love of God, not fear of His chastisements, that is bringing me into the cloister."

More than two years were required for making the arrangements concerning her children's future as well as her own. The business concluded, she offered herself to the Carmelites as a lay Sister and when this proposal was turned down she succeeded in getting a promise from the nuns to be allowed to do the work of a lay Sister.

She entered on April 20, 1674, when she was not yet thirty years old. That very day she asked the Novice Mistress to cut off her hair, and her request was granted. Six weeks later, so impressed were the community by her fervor, they clothed her in the holy habit. Bossuet, now her spiritual director, described her as "a miracle of grace." A year later her profession was fixed for June 4.

So dramatic a spectacle as the convent chapel presented on that bright summer morning has most probably never been seen. No country save France, no period save that of Louis the Fourteenth could have afforded it. All the world of rank and fashion attired in their most gorgeous finery assembled there on that unique occasion. (The King had the good taste and the good sense to leave Paris for the day.) All eyes were fixed on the door through which Sister Louise de la Misericorde was to enter. On the stroke of the appointed hour there appeared first Queen Marie Therese leading by the hand the repentant young woman, who for more than ten years had poisoned the Queen's cup of happiness and caused her the keenest pangs of wifely jealousy. At the other side of the Carmelite penitent walked the Princess de Longueville, known to all as a woman who had wasted her long-distant youth in profligacy and intrigue but, thanks to Sister Anne-Marie's intercession, had turned from her evil ways. Bossuet, of course, was the preacher. He took this text from the Apocalypse: "He that sat upon the throne said: Behold I make all things new."

During the sermon all eyes were on Sister Louise, who sat

motionless and with downcast gaze, between the saintly young Queen and the faded Princess, while great Bishop Bossuet strove with all the eloquence at his command to do justice to the triumph of divine grace of which the congregation were witnesses. Throughout the ceremony Sister Louise bore herself with the humility and simplicity natural to her; and, according to the famous letter writer, Madame de Sevigny, she had never looked more beautiful.

The austerities of Carmel were not severe enough to satisfy her thirst for suffering. All her life in religion she rose two hours earlier than did the community and spent this time in prayer before the Blessed Sacrament. A strong curb had to be kept on her use of instruments of penance. Unassisted by even a bowing acquaintance with the Latin tongue, she must have found choral recitation of the Divine Office a "sacrifice of praise" in real earnest.

Even in retirement she was much sought after, if occasionally by the merely curious more often by the sincerely devout, among whom was Queen Marie Therese; nevertheless she discouraged visitors as firmly as courtesy would permit. Once when the Queen asked if she found Carmelite life easy, she replied, "Not easy, but it is the life I desire."

In the autumn of 1676 came news of the death of her brother, the Duke de la Valliere, Governor of the Province of Bourbonnais. Her nephew, knowing a message of sympathy would come to her from the King, took advantage of this opening to get her to obtain a favor for himself from his Majesty. Louise's nature was such that she preferred to send a petition to the King than a refusal to her brother's child. Louis granted it with these words: "If only I were fit to talk to so holy a nun I would offer her my condolences in person."

In the winter of 1679 all the courtiers, including Madame de Sevigny, intruded on her seclusion to congratulate her on the marriage of her daughter to the Prince de Conti. The famous letter writer reports the affair as follows:

> Sister Louise adapts her style perfectly to her black veil, and mingles her maternal tenderness with that suitable to a bride of Christ. The King marries off her daughter as if Marianne were the Queen's child being wed to the King of Spain! He is giving her a royal dowry of five hundred thousand gold crowns, the usual one for a Princess of the Blood – with this difference that these will be paid whereas the others seldom do more than grace the contract. When I saw Sister Louise [who was thirty-five at the time] she looked like an angel; she retains all her old beauty. I thought her neither puffy nor yellow. She is not so slim as formerly and looks happier. She has just the same wonderful eyes and the same way of looking at you. Austerity, bad food and want of sleep have not made her eyes sunken or dim and the queer habit does not in the least lessen her gracefulness or her poise. She spoke very pleasantly to me. Her son-in-law, the Prince, regards her with deep affection and respect and has made her his spiritual director.

Four years later on the death of her sixteen-year-old son, the Duke of Vermandois, only one eminent figure from the world of Paris called to see her – Bossuet, who had been asked to break the sad news to her. At first her mother's heart found vent in sobs and tears but soon controlling her emotion she said: "I ought to weep on account of his birth rather than on account of his death," and after a few minutes' further conversation she went to choir to find relief in praying for her dead child.

The finest hour of her life came in the year 1685 when she met in the parlor an unexpected visitor. It was none other than her supplanter. Madame de Montespan who, in her day of triumph, had treated Louise with unrelenting cruelty, now in her day of disgrace sought her out for support and consolation. And she was not disappointed. Hour after hour Sister Louise listened to the great lady's outpourings, reeking with self-pity, yet her large blue eyes expressed only the tenderest compassion, her soft voice only words of solace and encouragement. When she finally left, if she was not resigned to her dismissal from Court, at least she was comforted by the thought that in Sister Louise she had a true friend to whom she could confidently turn for sympathy and a patient hearing.

If Sister Louise asked permission to practice extra penances, she knew how to bear those that came her way through illness: quite simply she paid no heed to it. When erisypelas broke out on her leg, she bore the pain in silence; and not until her limping gait caught the Sister Infirmarian's attention was it discovered. When the Mother Prioress asked her why she had not reported that her leg was in this dreadful condition she replied: "But, Mother, I didn't know it was like that. I never looked at it."

The day before her death, though weak from illness, she rose as was her wont at three o'clock in the morning, but her strength failed her halfway down to the choir and a lay Sister found her in the corridor where she had fallen. She was carried to her cell and laid on her bed. The chaplain was sent for, and Sister Louise having received the Last Sacraments died peacefully. It was June 6, 1710. She was nearly sixty-six years old; she had spent thirty-seven years in Carmel. The hand of death smoothed out the lines on her face, restoring her old beauty and giving it the appearance of innocence regained.

Her only memorial is a couple of booklets she wrote in the hope of inspiring halfhearted Christians with the desire to taste and see that the Lord is sweet. Entitled "Reflections on the Mercy of God" and "Thoughts of a Penitent," they went into several editions and were in steady demand for more than a century after her death.

Chapter 8

There is much truth in the old proverb: "The best preacher is the heart, the best teacher is time, the best book is life, and the best friend is God." Time and life and her own affectionate heart taught Sister Anne-Marie that what human beings need is love and compassion and that the privilege of adulthood is to answer this need. She began with her immediate circle. From her first years in the cloister and all through the half century she passed there she did all in her power to please and help the Sisters, spreading around her an atmosphere of tranquillity and cordiality and in this way played her part in making the Carmel de Paris "a dovecote of the Virgin," "a paradise where the Lord could take His pleasure."

When her intimate friend, Anne de Montpensier, expressed astonishment at nuns living happily together though strictly enclosed and cut off from contact with other people, and asked Christine to tell her how she did it, she got this answer: "I realize that my Sisters in religion are the spouses of Christ." This sweet-minded and respectful attitude to each member of her community was the mellow fruit of the habit of judging others by her own sweet self. And it is certain that Sister Anne-Marie could not have made that reply had she not striven her hardest to become *adjutorium simile Sibi* – "a helpmate like to Himself" as well as to keep her plighted troth, her vows of religion.

The friend of her soul who seconded her endeavor to live up to the demands of her vocation was Mother Agnes de Bellefonds. It was she who had been sent from the Carmel de Paris to Bourges to act as Christine's support and adviser in her stand against her family. Naturally enough this experience forged between them a bond of intimacy that time only strengthened and drew closer. Her senior in religion by twenty years and in age by thirteen, she filled the office of prioress during the greater part of Sister Anne-Marie's life in Carmel and that of novice mistress during the period of Sister Anne-Marie's religious formation.

Mother Agnes' interest in her had been aroused at their first meeting many years earlier when five-year-old Christine came on a visit to the Faubourg St. Jacques. At sight of the motherless little girl, Sister Agnes' heart went out to her and she there and then prayed earnestly that God would one day bring her to the Carmel on a visit that would never end. Directly Christine had entered for good; she came under Mother Agnes' influence and for the next forty-three years, until death parted them, remained her loving and beloved disciple. In a letter to Mother Agnes, Bishop Bossuet, their mutual friend, wrote: "Do not let Sister Anne-Marie forget me before God. I always put you two together."

The older nun's love for the younger had never blinded her to her weaknesses. With infinite care and consideration she had applied the remedies and over the years experienced the deep joy of meeting with complete cooperation. Sister Anne-Marie on her side had unlimited confidence in Mother Agnes' judgment together with boundless respect for her intellectual gifts. Bossuet lost no opportunity of impressing on the younger nun her good fortune in having such a friend as Mother Agnes. Among the many women great as well as holy of his acquaintance he knew none to compare with her. What he admired most in her was the combination of characteristics rarely united in the same person: candor, prudence, compassion, and, surprisingly enough, appreciation in others of qualities she herself did not possess. For example, though herself by nature grave rather than gay she never underestimated the benefit in community life of minor graces such as charm and vivacity, manifest in no small degree in more than one of the nuns, among them Sister Anne-Marie. Bossuet, sixteen years younger than this great Carmelite, was, moreover, the busiest priest in Paris; yet he gave her lavishly of his time for he set great store by her opinion of spiritual matters knowing that it was based on mature reflection and experience.

Being one of the moving spirits of Catholicism's "second spring" in France he took advantage of his visits to the Carmelites to inform them of what the Church has a right to expect of her contemplatives, more especially at a period of renewal: concern that the Holy Spirit's guidance might prevail in the councils of churchmen. To this end, he told them, their most effective cooperation would consist in an ever more faithful following of His inspirations, more particularly those He has made crystal-clear in the New Testament: cultivation of the spirit of love, love of God, of neighbor, of the Church; cultivation of the spirit of truth, candor, sincerity, simplicity.

His eloquence was not lost on these two intimate friends of his. Consciously or unconsciously Mother Agnes picked up in handfuls the crumbs that fell from the great man's table and passed them on to the community in her Chapter homilies. However, toward the end of her life she dropped all her rhetoric and, concerned solely to bequeath them the sum total of good advice, she would say: "O my children, O my little children, love one another."

With the passage of the years Sister Anne-Marie's contact with the world by means of letters and conversations left her a prey to distressing reflections. From time to time old friends, saddened at the new trends in Parisian society, would bring her word of what seemed to her incredible changes in Court etiquette. Louis the Fourteenth's gentlemen of the bedchamber always genuflected when passing by his bed even when it was empty: at Mass the courtiers turned their backs to the altar and fixed their eyes on the King kneeling in the royal gallery so that it looked as if they came to church to worship their Sovereign while he was worshiping his God. Moreover, echoes of Jansenism, with its insidious fascination for minds given up to the contemplative life, resounded in the parlor, affecting Sister Anne-Marie so grievously that before going to Holy Communion she was sometimes taken with a fit of trembling. She was indebted to Mother Agnes for deliverance from the mental anguish brought on by reports of the religious controversies then raging in Paris, on which more than one cloistered community had come to grief. Drawing-room discussions on the subjects of grace and free-will were repeated to the Carmelites, and even they felt the pull of novelty in doctrine. Most serious of all, because most alluring, were the accounts of Quietism and Quietists that reached the convent parlor, but they stopped there – Bossuet saw to that. As his teaching on prayer influenced Sister Anne-Marie in no small measure, some specimen passages of it may not be out of place.

> The devotion of the present day seems to me faulty in one point, namely that people talk too much about their prayer and its special conditions. Instead of dwelling so much upon the

various stages of prayer it would be better simply to pray as God leads one, without fidgeting oneself to analyse and discuss so much. I see nothing tending to show that one is always in the same condition or that there is any fixed state of prayer; the Holy Spirit at one time casts the soul down, at another time lifts it up; now He seems to be leading it to perfection, and the next moment He brings it back where it was. Our business is to conform in all such changes to His leading and go in the direction He chooses.

When thoughts present themselves we should use them if they are good, and if a truth takes possession of the mind we must fix our heart upon it, turn it into practical resolutions and above all entreat God Who inspires us with it to enable us to bring it to good effect.

I think people make a great mistake in drawing so many fine distinctions concerning the Essence and Attributes of God. A prayer framed upon these definitions becomes very complex. In a word, true prayer and that which is best, lies in whatever unites us to God, whatever enables us to enjoy Him, to appreciate Him, to rejoice in His glory and to love Him as one's very own, so that, not satisfied with words or thoughts or affections or resolutions, one comes to a solid practice of detachment from self and from all created things.

Above all, it is desirable not to perplex the brain or over-excite the feelings, but to take that which comes within our spiritual grasp and to let ourselves be drawn gently to God. If we feel sensible consolation we may take it in passing, and as it flows by let ourselves be drawn in the very depths of our soul into God, loving Him Himself and not merely the pleasure we derive from Him, His truth rather than the satisfaction with which it fills us. Follow the path God opens to you without hesitation; do not desire a higher kind of prayer in order to be more closely united with God, but desire a higher and closer union with Him that He may fill and absorb you more and more, that you may be as wholly His by your own will as you are in right of creation and redemption.

The great and only proof that our prayer is good is a changed life. The object of prayer is not to make us spend some interesting hours each day in God's company but rather to make our life a new and better thing.

The beatitude of peacemakers was enjoyed by Sister Anne-

Marie throughout the continual warfare in seventeenth-century France, including the long-drawn-out Civil War. In this fratricidal strife, the leaders on both sides being cousins of hers (the Great Condé and his deformed brother, the Prince de Conti) she could not be indifferent to the vicissitudes of the conflict, bewildering though they were. In the political chaos of the time many of her relatives were gravely affected in both fame and fortune. Almost all of them, men as well as women, came to her to unburden their troubled breasts. True enough, her efforts to heal the divisions among them met with failure, yet she succeeded in passing on to them a share of the peace that reigned in her own heart. They went away consoled and — more important still — strengthened in the belief that the God who sets the limits to the tides of the sea, says: "Thus far and no farther" to the waves of war.

If the state of the country called for the prayer and penance of saints so did the condition of the clergy: at that time the word "priest" was a term of contempt. Her mind steeped in the lore of the Bible, she needed no reminder of the necessity and the power of the intercession of God's friends. A thoroughly apostolic contemplative, she did her part in this work of obtaining grace for the graceless, especially for those with the claims of kinship upon her. Nevertheless it must be added that her prayers did not always bring about the desired result. Whereas her cousin, the Great Condé, made a most Christian end, her ecclesiastical superior, Msgr. de Harlay, Archbishop of Paris, derived no visible benefit from her intercession: his death, if not precisely sudden, was certainly unprovided for. De la Baumalle* wrote of him: "Without a sign of repentance he breathed his last in the arms of his mistress."

* The name of De la Baumalle is coupled with that of the Duke de Saint-Simon on every list of the great diarists of the age of Louis XIV. This extract is taken from Vol. IV, p. 62 of his *Memories.*

Another cleric who, apparently, gained but little by her influence with God was related to her through her grandmother, la belle Gabrielle d'Estrées, his name being François-Annibal d'Estrées. Though the validly consecrated Bishop of Noyon, he developed a taste for soldiering, abandoned his sacred calling, demanded military training, and eventually rose to the rank of a marshal of France. He earned the gratitude of the monks of the Grande Chartreuse by presenting them with the formula of one of their liqueurs.

Through all the last thirty years of her life her ailing body became for her an instrument of penance much more crucifying than any hair shirt, any chain. Attacks of arthritis became almost incessant and it was only by dint of sheer willpower that she managed to drag herself through her arduous day, both in winter and in summer. When the pain in her legs got so severe that she could not walk, the doctor asked the Prioress to make the patient wear fur-lined clothes. Mother Agnes would willingly have provided them but on telling Sister Anne-Marie of his orders she was met by a storm of protest: "What, Mother! Surely you don't wish me to break the Constitutions! I would rather die of pain than dress myself up in furs." When her hands became badly affected she was reduced to a state of near helplessness; nevertheless she assisted at Mass each morning and forced herself to go through the rest of the Carmelite day. Nothing short of the ailment described by the doctor as "contraction of the nerves" could get her to stay in bed all day. Occasionally there would come a respite of a few weeks and then, regardless of the Prioress' considerate warnings not to overtax her strength, she would resume attendance at all community exercises.

Ever since that feast of Our Lady of Mount Carmel, 1646, when our Lord had invited her to spend her life with Him

He had been for her "the Only One" and this noblest of passions attained its highest intensity in the pain-filled closing years of her life. Every aggravation of her suffering brought with it a keener realization of the physical and mental anguish borne by her divine Spouse for love of her, and as the various parts of her body succumbed to disease she would remind herself of the various sufferings of Jesus in His Passion. Her patience was rewarded by the supreme grace of the love of the Cross so that no complaint ever fell from her lips, not even when she saw herself a burden to others. Polite inquiries after her health were gently turned aside by her own expressions of sympathy and concern for her fellow sufferers in the infirmary. And she liked to give a humorous or pleasant turn to the disagreeables of the sickroom. For instance she would toss off a cup of medicine as if it were a glass of champagne and make fun of herself as she hobbled along the corridors with the aid of a stick, twirling it gaily if she could do so without risk of stumbling. She was also a martyr to skin disease together with a strange form of general inflammation. When this latter trouble attacked her gums causing severe toothache she used to quote this verse of Psalm 57 with a merry twinkle in her eye: "God shall break in pieces their teeth in their mouth. The Lord shall break the grinders of the lions."

The year 1693 brought her the news of the grave illness and, three weeks later, the death of her girlhood's dearest friend, Anne de Montpensier. In her sixty-five years, life had brought La Grande Mademoiselle many disillusionments, the most tragic of them all at the hands of the Duke de Lauzun (the soldier who had fumbled the French military expedition to Ireland in 1690). In her need of solace she always bent her steps in the direction of the Faubourg St. Jacques where, while reminiscing and moralizing with her beloved Christine, she never failed to find strength and consolation.

The death of Mother Agnes was the last and, perhaps, the most poignant sorrow of Sister Anne-Marie's whole life. It brought on a marked disimprovement in her already enfeebled condition and although she survived Mother Agnes by almost ten years it is true in a sense that she never got over her death. At mention of Mother Agnes' name tears would stream down her face. The young nuns were shocked at what they took to be her lack of detachment. She let them put on it whatever construction they chose: how could they understand the weakness and the loneliness of old age? All her other friends were dead and she made no new ones. It was during these last years, however, when everything failed her that she enjoyed the deepest peace of soul she had ever known, her solitariness being filled with the divine presence. One day a young nun, struck by the expression of serenity on Sister Anne-Marie's face, said to her: "Don't you think your long years of prayer and penance will obtain for you a great reward?" To which the old nun replied: "Nothing of the kind, child. It is from the pure mercy of God that I expect everything."

Her disease taking a decisive turn for the worse, she permitted herself to make just one request – to have placed near her bed pictures of our Lord in the various stages of His Passion so that when her pain became intolerable she might draw courage from the sight of His sufferings. And many an evening with the onset of darkness she was overheard murmuring appropriate verses from the Psalms, most frequently this one: "In Thy light I shall see light."

Before death came, her tranquil solitude, so often gladdened by a sense of the nearness of God, underwent a terrifying change. The Spirit led her soul into that dark, mysterious region where God's special friends go through the final stage of their growth in Christ, an experience corresponding to His sense of dereliction on the Cross. All her former love of Jesus Christ became to her as unreal as a dream. She felt as if God had gone away and left her to herself, left her to an experimental knowledge of the truth that without Him she could do nothing, that without Him she was nothing. From out these depths she sent up the piteous cries of Psalm 87:

> Lord God, day and night I cry bitterly to thee, let my prayer reach thy presence, give audience to my entreaty, for indeed my heart is full of trouble. My life sinks ever closer to the grave; I count as one of those that go down into the abyss like one powerless. As well lie among the dead, men laid low in the grave, men thou rememberest no longer, cast away now from thy protecting hand. Such is the place where thou hast laid me, in a deep pit where the dark waters swirl. . . . I lie in a prison whence there is no escape, my eyes grow dim with tears. On thee I call, to thee stretch out my hands, each day that passes. . . . How can there be talk of thy marvels in a world of darkness, of thy favor in a land where all is forgotten? To prayer, Lord, I fall heartily, it shall reach thee while there is yet time. Why dost thou reject my plea, Lord, and turn thy face away from me? . . . Friends and neighbors gone, a world of shadows is all my company.

Then the dread of death seized upon her. Death, the thought of which used to be the secret joy of her heart, now assumed the loathsome aspect of extinction. Afraid of death and afraid of life, she scarcely knew how to pray. One unrecognized consolation remained to her, namely, faith, belief in the existence of God. She wanted God, therefore she had God: "Though I walk through the valley of the shadow of death I shall fear no evil for thou art with me." This verse of Psalm 22 was constantly on her lips, in her heart. This trial did not continue long but its severity would seem to have sapped the last remnants of her vitality.

Holy Mass had always been the center of her day, the inspiration of her life in Christ, as a note in her own handwriting testifies: "This morning after Communion I felt the presence of our Lord as never before. I saw in a new light the significance of the Eucharist as the memorial of His Passion. I understood that I, too, must be a victim consumed with love in Him and through Him. Feeling as if all my attachments to this world had snapped, I begged Him to take me to Himself. Then the contrast between my Divine Bridegroom and myself gave me pause, He infinitely loving and perfect, I utterly selfish and sinful, and so I told Him I am willing to live as long as He pleases." He did not keep her waiting long; it was His good pleasure to call her to Himself, August 22, 1701. On the evening of the twenty-first, sensing that her end was near she asked for and received the Last Anointings and Holy Viaticum. With break of day, she began counting the hours to Mass time; she wanted to be present at the Holy Sacrifice on the last day of her life. Though her physical powers had reached their limit, she had herself carried to the tribune from which a clear view of the altar could be had. At the Consecration when the Sacred Host was lifted up, our Lord's words: "If I be lifted up, I will draw all to Myself," came to her mind and she prayed that she might be one of these that very day. Back in her cell the weakness of death settled on her. The infirmarian watching at her bedside noticed from hour to hour the increasing irregularity of the breathing, the pallor spreading across the face, the expression of full consciousness. Just before the end the watcher saw the lips move soundlessly. Bending down to catch the last words of her whom she regarded as a saint, she distinctly heard Sister Anne-Marie say: "O God, thou wilt not despise a humble and contrite heart" (Ps 50).

So passed away Anne-Louise-Christine de Foix de la Valette

d'Epernon, the Pompilia of the Bourbons, "white enough for three." In the eyes of the world she ranked as the last and the least of the House of Epernon, but in the light of heaven is its enduring glory.